Between the Lines

To the man on the 7.22 a.m.
from Kilbarrack

Between the Lines

Poems on the DART

JONATHAN WILLIAMS
EDITOR

THE LILLIPUT PRESS
MCMXCIV

First published in 1994 by
THE LILLIPUT PRESS LTD
4 Rosemount Terrace, Arbour Hill,
Dublin 7, Ireland.

A CIP record for this
title is available from
The British Library.

ISBN 1 874675 39 2

Cover design & layout by Raymond Kyne
Cover illustration Gillian Reidy
Set in 10 on 20 Walbaum
Printed in Dublin by ßetaprint

Contents

Introduction

In May 1986, after nine years away from Ireland, I first stepped into a DART train, finding it a 'clean, well-lighted place' after the subways of New York and Chicago. Four months before, in London, Poems on the Underground had been launched, and the sight of those first poems on the District line made me long to do the same for Dublin on my return. Soon, with the enthusiastic collaboration of Raymond Kyne and Jim and Marianne Mays, Poetry in Motion was formed; the *raison d'être* of the scheme was to make poetry available to those who, otherwise, might have too little time, or even inclination, to read it.

The first two Poems on the DART went up in January 1987. Displaying the work of Irish poets would be a primary consideration. 'Beautiful Lofty Things', by W.B. Yeats, was chosen because of its reference to 'Maud Gonne at Howth station waiting a train'. The second—a ninth-century nature poem in Irish, with a translation by Thomas Kinsella—is typical of many glosses found in the margins of monastic manuscripts, and signalled our commitment to presenting work in the Irish language.

Unlike our London counterparts, who from time to time put up extracts from long poems—Milton's 'Paradise Lost' and Keats's 'Endymion', for instance, we decided to display only complete poems, doubtless intimidated by the entire body of world poetry on which we could draw. (The single exception—discovered too late!—is Edmund Waller's 'Old Age', which derives from the last two stanzas of 'Of the Last Verses in the Book', *Poems* [1686].) Our graphic designer, Raymond Kyne, established an upper limit of fourteen or (occasionally) fifteen lines, whilst retaining legibility, and this enabled us to include the sonnet. We had made our Procrustean bed and now would have to lie on it.

Immediately it became clear that the work of some fine poets would have to be jettisoned because they wrote so sparingly in the short form; but this, ironically, proved a blessing because it helped us to whittle down the vast range of literature open to us.

The poems in *Between the Lines* exhibit, we hope, a variety of moods, subject matter and tones. The eternal themes—love, death, war, the passage of time, memory, the seasons, the natural world—are represented; others were put up to mark particular events or occasions. These include the centenaries of the births of T.S. Eliot, Osip Mandelstam and Francis Ledwidge; the Dublin Millennium in 1988; separate visits to Dublin by Joseph Brodsky and Derek Walcott, who both read (Brodsky in Russian and English) their poems in trains in Dún Laoghaire station; Randall Jarrell's scornful lullaby coincided with the deployment of American troops in the Kuwaiti desert; and during Dublin's year as European City of Culture, in 1991, we presented the work of two living poets from each member state of the European Community, in Catalan, Danish, Dutch, French, German, Greek, Irish, Italian, Portuguese, Scots Gaelic, Spanish and Welsh, and in English translation.

From the start, we resolved that half our bi-monthly selection of eight poems would be by Irish poets, but otherwise we have no manifesto, no literary axes to grind. The essential criterion is that the poems will cause a smile, give comfort, disturb, provoke, or simply entertain. The impulse is to set these poems free from the books in which they are locked, often unread by the tens of thousands of DART travellers. Exceptions were Seamus Heaney, Craig Raine and Hugh Maxton, who wrote expressly for Poems on the DART.

Encouragement arrived in letters from the public, commenting on individual lines and praising favourite poems. A few items of correspondence stand out: a postcard, written on the journey south out of Dublin and mailed in Bray, from a woman moved by Christina Rossetti's 'Remember'; two separate requests for the words of Anne Brontë's 'Farewell' (many months after it had been taken down), so that they could be incised on the gravestones of people who had died tragically young; a man who had remembered only the last line of Derek Walcott's 'To Norline' (again months after its removal), who wanted to have the full poem; and many letters requesting copies of the original DART cards (the concrete poems by John Updike and Ian Hamilton Finlay were especially popular).

Whether or not we have chosen the best short poem by any of these poets is a matter for others to determine. With some, there was a lot of wavering. Which poems by Hardy, Frost and Joyce, which Shakespeare sonnet, should go up in the carriages? In these and in other cases, we canvassed widely, and we never resisted picking a poem that might be well known to many passengers; there are always new readers to win over.

So far, no poet has appeared more than once, unless he or she is represented by the translation of another poet, yet there are legions still to come: Ben Jonson, Swift, Wordsworth, Housman, de la Mare, Miroslav

Holub, Tony Harrison, and a slew of new Irish poets. In future years, with the continued support of Cyril Ferris and Iarnród Eireann, we would like to give space to voices from the Caribbean, Africa and Canada, and perhaps to display over one two-month period poems for, and even by, children.

Between the Lines contains roughly three-quarters of the nearly 200 poems that have journeyed from Bray to Howth and back, presented in the order in which they appeared in the trains. Liberated for a couple of months from the confines of the printed page, they are now returned to where they traditionally belong.

JONATHAN WILLIAMS
Sandycove, County Dublin
November 1994

Between the Lines

Beautiful Lofty Things

Beautiful lofty things: O'Leary's noble head;

My father upon the Abbey stage, before him a raging
   crowd:

'This Land of Saints,' and then as the applause died out,

'Of plaster Saints'; his beautiful mischievous head
   thrown back.

Standish O'Grady supporting himself between the tables

Speaking to a drunken audience high nonsensical words;

Augusta Gregory seated at her great ormolu table,

Her eightieth winter approaching: 'Yesterday he
   threatened my life.

I told him that nightly from six to seven I sat at this table,

The blinds drawn up'; Maud Gonne at Howth station
   waiting a train,

Pallas Athene in that straight back and arrogant head:

All the Olympians; a thing never known again.

W.B. Yeats

Int en gaires asin tsail

alainn guilbnen as glan gair:

rinn binn buide fir duib druin:

cas cor cuirther, guth ind luin.

Anonymous

2

A bird is calling from the willow

with lovely beak, a clean call.

Sweet yellow tip; he is black and strong.

It is doing a dance, the blackbird's song.

Translation by Thomas Kinsella

The brain is wider than the sky,

> For, put them side by side,

The one the other will include

> With ease, and you beside.

The brain is deeper than the sea,

> For, hold them, blue to blue,

The one the other will absorb,

> As sponges, buckets do.

The brain is just the weight of God,

> For, lift them, pound for pound,

And they will differ, if they do,

> As syllable from sound.

Emily Dickinson

Talking in Bed

Talking in bed ought to be easiest,
Lying together there goes back so far,
An emblem of two people being honest.

Yet more and more time passes silently.
Outside, the wind's incomplete unrest
Builds and disperses clouds about the sky,

And dark towns heap up on the horizon.
None of this cares for us. Nothing shows why
At this unique distance from isolation

It becomes still more difficult to find
Words at once true and kind,
Or not untrue and not unkind.

Philip Larkin

Gaineamh shúraic

A chroí, ná lig dom is mé ag dul a chodladh
titim isteach sa phluais dhorcha.
Tá eagla orm roimh an ngaineamh shúraic,
roimh na cuasa scamhaite amach ag uisce,
áiteanna ina luíonn móin faoin dtalamh.

Thíos ann tá giúis is bogdéil ársa;
tá cnámha na bhFiann 'na luí go sámh ann
a gclaimhte gan mheirg—is cailín báite,
rópa cnáibe ar a muinéal tairrice.

Tá sé anois ina lag trá rabharta,
tá gealach lán is trá mhór ann,
is anocht nuair a chaithfead mo shúile a dhúnadh
bíodh talamh slán, bíodh gaineamh chruaidh romham.

Nuala Ní Dhomhnaill

6

Quicksand

My love, don't let me, going to sleep

fall into the dark cave.

I fear the sucking sand

I fear the eager hollows in the water,

places with bogholes underground.

Down there there's ancient wood and bogdeal:

the Fianna's bones are there at rest

with rustless swords—and a drowned girl,

a noose around her neck.

Now there is a weak ebb-tide:

the moon is full, the sea will leave the land

and tonight when I close my eyes

let there be terra firma, let there be hard sand.

Translation by Michael Hartnett

Sic Vita

Like to the falling of a star,
Or as the flights of eagles are,
Or like the fresh spring's gaudy hue,
Or silver drops of morning dew,
Or like a wind that chafes the flood,
Or bubbles which on water stood:
Even such is man, whose borrowed light
Is straight called in, and paid to night.

The wind blows out, the bubble dies;
The spring entombed in autumn lies;
The dew dries up, the star is shot;
The flight is past: and man forgot.

Henry King

Roundelay

on all that strand

at end of day

steps sole sound

long sole sound

until unbidden stay

then no sound

on all that strand

long no sound

until unbidden go

steps sole sound

long sole sound

on all that strand

at end of day

Samuel Beckett

Prelude

Still south I went and west and south again,
Through Wicklow from the morning till the night,
And far from cities, and the sites of men,
Lived with the sunshine and the moon's delight.

I knew the stars, the flowers, and the birds,
The grey and wintry sides of many glens,
And did but half remember human words,
In converse with the mountains, moors, and fens.

John M. Synge

Dublin 4

Lit carriages ran through our fields at night

Like promises being speedily withdrawn.

Awakened by train-noise, well-placed, suburban,

I ask myself is this where they were going.

Seamus Heaney

Mirror

When you look

into a mirror

it is not

yourself you see,

but a kind

of apish error

posed in fearful

symmetry.

John Updike

Remember

Remember me when I am gone away,

    Gone far away into the silent land;

    When you can no more hold me by the hand,

Nor I half turn to go yet turning stay.

Remember me when no more day by day

    You tell me of our future that you planned:

    Only remember me; you understand

It will be late to counsel then or pray.

Yet if you should forget me for a while

    And afterwards remember, do not grieve:

    For if the darkness and corruption leave

    A vestige of the thoughts that once I had,

Better by far you should forget and smile

    Than that you should remember and be sad.

Christina Rossetti

Not Waving But Drowning

Nobody heard him, the dead man,
But still he lay moaning:
I was much further out than you thought
And not waving but drowning.

Poor chap, he always loved larking
And now he's dead
It must have been too cold for him his heart gave way,
They said.

Oh, no no no, it was too cold always
(Still the dead one lay moaning)
I was much too far out all my life
And not waving but drowning.

Stevie Smith

Corner Seat

Suspended in a moving night
The face in the reflected train
Looks at first sight as self-assured
As your own face—But look again:

Windows between you and the world
Keep out the cold, keep out the fright;
Then why does your reflection seem
So lonely in the moving night?

Louis MacNeice

Uaigneas

Blas sméara dubha
tar éis báistí
ar bharr an tsléibhe.

I dtost an phríosúin
feadaíl fhuar na traenach.

Cogar gháire beirt leannán
don aonarán.

Brendan Behan

Loneliness

The tang of blackberries
wet with rain
on the hilltop.

In the silence of the prison
the clear whistle of the train.

The happy whisperings of lovers
to the lonely one.

Brendan Behan

Anecdote of the Jar

I placed a jar in Tennessee,
And round it was, upon a hill.
It made the slovenly wilderness
Surround that hill.

The wilderness rose up to it,
And sprawled around, no longer wild.
The jar was round upon the ground
And tall and of a port in air.

It took dominion everywhere.
The jar was gray and bare.
It did not give of bird or bush,
Like nothing else in Tennessee.

Wallace Stevens

Fire and Ice

Some say the world will end in fire,
Some say in ice.
From what I've tasted of desire
I hold with those who favor fire.
But if it had to perish twice,
I think I know enough of hate
To say that for destruction ice
Is also great
And would suffice.

Robert Frost

I May, I Might, I Must

If you will tell me why the fen

appears impassable, I then

will tell you why I think that I

can get across it if I try.

Marianne Moore

A Part of Speech

I was born and grew up in the Baltic marshland
by zinc-grey breakers that always marched on
in twos. Hence all rhymes, hence that wan flat voice
that ripples between them like hair still moist,
if it ripples at all. Propped on a pallid elbow,
the helix picks out of them no sea rumble
but a clap of canvas, of shutters, of hands, a kettle
on the burner, boiling—lastly, the seagull's metal
cry. What keeps hearts from falseness in this flat region
is that there is nowhere to hide and plenty of room for
   vision.
Only sound needs echo and dreads its lack.
A glance is accustomed to no glance back.

Joseph Brodsky

Ar Aíocht Dom

A ardchathair ársa ár dtíre!

Lán mo choise bainim coitianta

As cosáin do shráideanna

Ach torann níor bhaineas astu

Mar a dhéanfadh fear a déarfadh

Gur leis féin tú ó cheart sinsir:

Is do mo ghoid féin a bhímse

Trí na mílte faoi mar is cuí don té

Ar strainséir é is aoi ar d'ucht.

Máirtín Ó Direáin

A Melancholy Love

Part elegant and partly slum,
Skies cleaned by rain,
Plum-blue hills for a background:
Dublin, of course.
The only city that has lodged
Sadly in my bones.

Sheila Wingfield

Liffey Bridge

I gazed along the waters at the West,

Watching the low sky colour into flame,

Until each narrowing steeple I could name

Grew dark as the far vapours, and my breast

With silence like a sorrow was possessed.

And men as moving shadows went and came;

The smoke that stained the sunset seemed like shame,

Or lust, or some great evil unexpressed.

Then with a longing for the taintless air,

I called that desolation back again,

Which reigned when Liffey's widening banks were bare;

Before Ben Edair gazed upon the Dane,

Before the Hurdle Ford, and long before

Finn drowned the young men by its meadowy shore.

Oliver St John Gogarty

Fin

I know it's the end.

I can see it coming. I'm

like those women in the cinema who make you mad

fumbling for gloves

elbowing themselves into coats, buttoning up—

such a final snapping shut of handbags

the minute it looks like it's all over

but a change of mood and music.

So you demand response do you

right to the bitter end, you like

to see the credits roll?

I'm off.

Liz Lochhead

Séasúir

Bailc shamhraidh sna cnoic—
i dtitim throm thréan na fearthainne
cloisim míle bó bainne á mblí.

I mbáine an gheimhridh sna cnoic
bíonn na bunsoip trom le sioc—
as a gcuid siní sileann tost.

Cathal Ó Searcaigh

Seasons

A summer squall on the hills—

out of the strong downpour of rain

I can hear a thousand milking cows.

In the whiteness of winter hills

thatch-eaves are heavy with frost—

in their teats, mere drops of stillness.

Translation by Thomas McCarthy

The Sick Rose

O Rose, thou art sick!
  The invisible worm,
That flies in the night,
  In the howling storm,

Has found out thy bed
  Of crimson joy;
And his dark secret love
  Does thy life destroy.

William Blake

Farewell

Farewell to Thee! But not farewell

To all my fondest thoughts of Thee;

Within my heart they still shall dwell

And they shall cheer and comfort me.

Life seems more sweet that Thou didst live

And men more true that Thou wert one;

Nothing is lost that Thou didst give,

Nothing destroyed that Thou hast done.

Anne Brontë

Night Train

Moths go over and over the glass,
puffs of French chalk,
like someone checking for fingerprints.

Between two barbed wire fences,
on the verge of the underworld,
the train is arrested. Irrevocable

as a declaration of love,
this silent, stolen masterpiece,
this aching gallery of gilded light

we would now like to leave.

Craig Raine

Prelude

The winter evening settles down
With smell of steaks in passageways.
Six o'clock.
The burnt-out ends of smoky days.
And now a gusty shower wraps
The grimy scraps
Of withered leaves about your feet
And newspapers from vacant lots;
The showers beat
On broken blinds and chimney-pots,
And at the corner of the street
A lonely cab-horse steams and stamps.
And then the lighting of the lamps.

T.S. Eliot

The Emigrant Irish

Like oil lamps we put them out the back,

of our houses, of our minds. We had lights

better than, newer than and then

a time came, this time and now

we need them. Their dread, makeshift example.

They would have thrived on our necessities.

What they survived we could not even live.

By their lights now it is time to

imagine how they stood there, what they stood with,

that their possessions may become our power.

Cardboard. Iron. Their hardships parcelled in them.

Patience. Fortitude. Long-suffering

in the bruise-coloured dusk of the New World.

And all the old songs. And nothing to lose.

Eavan Boland

Cock-Crow

Out of the wood of thoughts that grows by night
To be cut down by the sharp axe of light,—
Out of the night, two cocks together crow,
Cleaving the darkness with a silver blow:
And bright before my eyes twin trumpeters stand,
Heralds of splendour, one at either hand,
Each facing each as in a coat of arms:
The milkers lace their boots up at the farms.

Edward Thomas

Rousseau na Gaeltachta

Lig di, adúirt an file,
is ná smachtaigh í,
níl inti seo ach gearrchaile
is is breoiteacht é an t-eagla
a chrapann an nádúr.

Lig di, adúirt an file,
is ná smachtaigh í,
lig di fás gan bac ar bith
go dtína haoirde cheapaithe,
tá an t-aer fós bog os a cionn.

Seán Ó Tuama

A Gaeltacht Rousseau

Let her be, said the poet;

do not chastise her,

she is still a stripling

and fear is a sickness

that stunts all human growth.

Let her be, said the poet;

do not chastise her,

let her grow unimpeded

to whatever height she is meant for:

the air is still soft above her head.

Seán Ó Tuama

The Eagle

He clasps the crag with crookèd hands;
Close to the sun in lonely lands,
Ring'd with the azure world, he stands.

The wrinkled sea beneath him crawls;
He watches from his mountain walls,
And like a thunderbolt he falls.

Alfred, Lord Tennyson

The Boundary Commission

You remember that village where the border ran
Down the middle of the street,
With the butcher and baker in different states?
Today he remarked how a shower of rain

Had stopped so cleanly across Golightly's lane
It might have been a wall of glass
That had toppled over. He stood there, for ages,
To wonder which side, if any, he should be on.

Paul Muldoon

The Cocks

All night the water has worked without pause.
The rain has burnt its linseed oil till morning.
And steam rolls from beneath the lilac lid.
The earth smokes like a pot of cabbage soup.

And when the shaken grass springs up again,
who will express my terror to the dew
at that hour when a cock begins to bawl,
another after him, then all the rest?

Examining each several year by name,
each in his turn they call upon the dark
and so begin their prophecy of change
in rain, in earth, in love, in all, in all.

Boris Pasternak
Translation by J.M. Cohen

Last Hill in a Vista

Come, let us tell the weeds in ditches
How we are poor, who once had riches,
And lie out in the sparse and sodden
Pastures that the cows have trodden,
The while an autumn night seals down
The comforts of the wooden town.

Come, let us counsel some cold stranger
How we sought safety, but loved danger.
So, with stiff walls about us, we
Chose this more fragile boundary:
Hills, where light poplars, the firm oak,
Loosen into a little smoke.

Louise Bogan

Pharao's Daughter

In Agypt's land contaygious to the Nile,
Old Pharao's daughter went to bathe in style,
She tuk her dip and came unto the land,
And for to dry her royal pelt she ran along the strand:

A bull-rush tripped her, whereupon she saw
A smiling babby in a wad of straw,
She took it up and said in accents mild,
'Tare-an-ages, girls, which o' yees own the child?'

Michael Moran ('Zozimus')

Chinese Winter

From these bare trees

The sticks of last year's nests

Print sad characters against the moon;

While wind-blown moonlight,

Stripping fields to silver,

Scrawls December on each frozen pool.

Light washed on every tree

Roots it in black shadow,

As last year's love now roots me in black night;

And where love danced

Footprints of fiery moments

Flash out memorials in silent ice.

F.R. Higgins

Flowers by the Sea

When over the flowery, sharp pasture's
edge, unseen, the salt ocean

lifts its form—chicory and daisies
tied, released, seem hardly flowers alone

but color and the movement—or the shape
perhaps—of restlessness, whereas

the sea is circled and sways
peacefully upon its plantlike stem

William Carlos Williams

To My Daughter Betty

In wiser days, my darling rosebud, blown

To beauty proud as was your Mother's prime.

In that desired, delayed, incredible time,

You'll ask why I abandoned you, my own,

And the dear heart that was your baby throne,

To dice with death. And oh! they'll give you rhyme

And reason: some will call the thing sublime,

And some decry it in a knowing tone.

So here, while the mad guns curse overhead,

And tired men sigh with mud for couch and floor,

Know that we fools, now with the foolish dead,

Died not for flag, nor King, nor Emperor,

But for a dream, born in a herdsman's shed,

And for the secret Scripture of the poor.

Thomas Kettle

Boy Bathing

On the edge of the springboard
A boy poses, columned light
Poised.
Seagulls crying wrinkles
The brown parchment cliffs.
His body shines: a knife!
Spread wings, he opens
Plunges
Through the gold glass of sunshine
Smashes
In crumbs of glass the silence.

Denis Devlin

A Dying Art

'That day would skin a fairy—
A dying art,' she said.
Not many left of the old trade.
Redundant and remote, they age
Gracefully in dark corners
With lamp-lighters, sail-makers
And native Manx speakers.

And the bone-handled knives with which
They earned their bread? My granny grinds
Her plug tobacco with one to this day.

Derek Mahon

Holy Sonnet

Death, be not proud, though some have called thee

Mighty and dreadful, for thou art not so;

For, those, whom thou think'st thou dost overthrow,

Die not, poor death, nor yet canst thou kill me.

From rest and sleep, which but thy pictures be,

Much pleasure, then from thee, much more must flow,

And soonest our best men with thee do go,

Rest of their bones, and soul's delivery.

Thou art slave to Fate, Chance, kings, and desperate men,

And dost with poison, war, and sickness dwell,

And poppy, or charms can make us sleep as well,

And better than thy stroke; why swell'st thou then?

One short sleep past, we wake eternally,

And death shall be no more; death, thou shalt die.

John Donne

A Farm Picture

Through the ample open door of the peaceful country barn,

A sunlit pasture field with cattle and horses feeding,

And haze and vista, and the far horizon fading away.

Walt Whitman

In the Middle of the Road

In the middle of the road there was a stone
there was a stone in the middle of the road
there was a stone
in the middle of the road there was a stone.

Never should I forget this event
in the life of my fatigued retinas.
Never should I forget that in the middle of the road
there was a stone
there was a stone in the middle of the road
in the middle of the road there was a stone.

Elizabeth Bishop
Translated from the Portuguese of
Carlos Drummond de Andrade

Sonnet 94

They that have power to hurt, and will do none,

That do not do the thing they most do show,

Who, moving others, are themselves as stone,

Unmoved, cold, and to temptation slow:

They rightly do inherit heaven's graces,

And husband nature's riches from expense,

They are the Lords and owners of their faces,

Others, but stewards of their excellence.

The summer's flower is to the summer sweet,

Though to itself, it only live and die,

But if that flower with base infection meet,

The basest weed outbraves his dignity:

    For sweetest things turn sourest by their deeds,

    Lilies that fester, smell far worse than weeds.

William Shakespeare

Double Negative

You were standing on the quay

Wondering who was the stranger on the mailboat

While I was on the mailboat

Wondering who was the stranger on the quay

Richard Murphy

To Norline

This beach will remain empty
for more slate-coloured dawns
of lines the surf continually
erases with its sponge,

and someone else will come
from the still-sleeping house,
a coffee mug warming his palm
as my body once cupped yours,

to memorize this passage
of a salt-sipping tern,
like when some line on a page
is loved, and it's hard to turn.

Derek Walcott

Reo

Maidin sheaca ghabhas amach
Is bhí seál póca romham ar sceach,
Rugas air le cur im phóca
Ach sciorr sé uaim mar bhí sé reoite:
Ní héadach beo a léim óm ghlaic
Ach rud fuair bás aréir ar sceach:
Is siúd ag taighde mé fé m'intinn
Go bhfuaireas macasamhail an ní seo—
 Lá dar phógas bean dem mhuintir
 Is í ina cónra reoite, sínte.

Seán Ó Ríordáin

Frozen

On a frosty morning I went out

And a handkerchief faced me on a bush.

I reached to put it in my pocket

But it slid from me for it was frozen.

No living cloth jumped from my grasp

But a thing that died last night on a bush,

And I went searching in my mind

Till I found its real equivalent:

The day I kissed a woman of my kindred

And she in the coffin, frozen, stretched.

Translation by Valentin Iremonger

Sonnet 15

An air which softens outlines, blurs horizons,
Hides mountain ranges until suddenly
The black peaks soar, steep, huge and sodden over
A valley where the stream and road are one.
In this land nothing's clear, no colour sharp
Except the green. The browns and reds and purples
Change sometimes by the minute with the moisture
Content of the air, as does the light.
The twilight lingers, bright but shadowless
Beyond the sunset. Since the sea surrounds
The whole, east light and west, north light and south
Are at the mercy of its mirror mass.
The south is sometimes clearer than the north
And ambiguity a law of life.

Anthony Cronin

Moonrise

I awoke in the Midsummer not-to-call night, in the
    white and the walk of the morning:
The moon, dwindled and thinned to the fringe of a
    fingernail held to the candle,
Or paring of paradisaïcal fruit, lovely in waning but
    lustreless,
Stepped from the stool, drew back from the barrow,
    of dark Maenefa the mountain;
A cusp still clasped him, a fluke yet fanged him,
    entangled him, not quite utterly.
This was the prized, the desirable sight, unsought,
    presented so easily,
Parted me leaf and leaf, divided me, eyelid and eyelid
    of slumber.

Gerard Manley Hopkins

Scholar

I splashed water on my face
And one glabrous drop
Ran down my neck and back
In a zig-zag chill.

As I climbed into bed,
Dazed with reading,
I felt the naked sheet
Sigh for the fool.

Sleep on the glazed eye,
Acrid paste on the tooth—
Is there a book that I
Would not burn for the truth?

Seamus Deane

Sonnet from the Portuguese XXII

When our two souls stand up erect and strong,
Face to face, silent, drawing nigh and nigher,
Until the lengthening wings break into fire
At either curvèd point,—what bitter wrong
Can the earth do to us, that we should not long
Be here contented? Think! In mounting higher,
The angels would press on us, and aspire
To drop some golden orb of perfect song
Into our deep, dear silence. Let us stay
Rather on earth, Belovèd,—where the unfit
Contrarious moods of men recoil away
And isolate pure spirits, and permit
A place to stand and love in for a day,
With darkness and the death-hour rounding it.

Elizabeth Barrett Browning

Home

A burst of sudden wings at dawn,
Faint voices in a dreamy noon,
Evenings of mist and murmurings,
And nights with rainbows of the moon.

And through these things a wood-way dim,
And waters dim, and slow sheep seen
On uphill paths that wind away
Through summer sounds and harvest green.

This is a song a robin sang
This morning on a broken tree,
It was about the little fields
That call across the world to me.

Francis Ledwidge

To My Dear and Loving Husband

If ever two were one, then surely we;

If ever man were lov'd by wife, then thee;

If ever wife was happy in a man,

Compare with me, ye women, if you can.

I prize thy love more than whole mines of gold,

Or all the riches that the East doth hold.

My love is such that rivers cannot quench,

Nor aught but love from thee give recompense.

Thy love is such I can no way repay;

The heavens reward thee manifold, I pray.

Then while we live, in love lets so persever,

That when we live no more, we may live ever.

Anne Bradstreet

Leannáin

idir cnoc is sliabh

in iarthar an domhain

mhaireadar ó lá go lá

a scartha

idir an dá linn

fásann fiúise

dúisíonn na clocha

tagann an fharraige arís

Michael Davitt

Lovers

between hill and mountain

in the western world

they lived from day to day

of separation

in the meantime

fuchsia grows

the stones are roused

the tide flows again

Translation by Philip Casey

Four Ducks on a Pond

Four ducks on a pond,

A grass-bank beyond,

A blue sky of spring,

White clouds on the wing;

What a little thing

To remember for years—

To remember with tears!

William Allingham

The Oil Lamp

I hear the bamboo creak like a cracked joint
Although the terrace stays so still-life still.
The oil lamp's blade is pared to a fine point
And purrs inside its glass. A long tendril
Wavers like a signal from its clouded stack.
The crickets tune non-stop their lost waveband
Deciphering a code they cannot crack
With only one glazed star to lend a hand ...
A still scenario a good painter could
Catch all the silence in but not that creak
That has the nervy twang of brittle wood.
With a deep breath the decamped wind is back.
I look in at the window with a start:
The lantern's blade is jabbing at my heart.

Rory Brennan

Heaviness and tenderness—sisters: the same features.

Bees and wasps suck the heavy rose.

Man dies, heat leaves the sand, the sun

of yesterday is borne on a black stretcher.

Oh the heavy honeycomb, the tender webs—easier

to hoist a stone than to say your name!

Only one purpose is left me, but it is golden:

to free myself of the burden, time.

I drink the roiled air like a dark water.

Time has been plowed; the rose was earth. In a slow

whirlpool the heavy tender roses,

rose heaviness, rose tenderness, are plaited in double wreaths.

Osip Mandelstam

Translation by Clarence Brown and W.S. Merwin

Secrecy

Had we been only lovers from a book
That holy men, who had a hand in heaven,
Illuminated: in a yellow wood,
Where crimson beast and bird are clawed with gold
And, wound in branches, hunt or hawk themselves,
Sun-woman, I would hide you as the ring
Of his own shining fetters that the snake,
Who is the wood itself, can never find.

Austin Clarke

Cré na Mná Tí

Coinnibh an teaghlach geal
Agus an chlann fé smacht,
Nigh agus sciúr agus glan,
Cóirigh proinn agus lacht,
Iompaigh tochta, leag brat,
Ach, ar nós Sheicheiriseáide,
Ní mór duit an fhilíocht chomh maith!

Máire Mhac an tSaoi

The Housewife's Credo

Keep the dwelling bright and the children in order;

wash and scour and clean; prepare meal and beverage;

turn mattress—spread cloth—but, like

Scheherazade, you will need to write poetry also!

Máire Mhac an tSaoi

A Lullaby

For wars his life and half a world away
The soldier sells his family and days.
He learns to fight for freedom and the State;
He sleeps with seven men within six feet.

He picks up matches and he cleans out plates;
Is lied to like a child, cursed like a beast.
They crop his head, his dog tags ring like sheep
As his stiff limbs shift wearily to sleep.

Recalled in dreams or letters, else forgot,
His life is smothered like a grave, with dirt;
And his dull torment mottles like a fly's
The lying amber of the histories.

Randall Jarrell

Heredity

I am the family face;

Flesh perishes, I live on,

Projecting trait and trace

Through time to times anon,

And leaping from place to place

Over oblivion.

The years-heired feature that can

In curve and voice and eye

Despise the human span

Of durance—that is I;

The eternal thing in man,

That heeds no call to die.

Thomas Hardy

Pygmalion's Image

Not only her stone face, laid back staring in the ferns,

But everything the scoop of the valley contains begins to move

(And beyond the horizon the trucks beat the highway).

A tree inflates gently on the curve of the hill;

An insect crashes on the carved eyelid;

Grass blows westward from the roots,

As the wind knifes under her skin and ruffles it like a book.

The crisp hair is real, wriggling like snakes;

A rustle of veins, tick of blood in the throat;

The lines of the face tangle and catch, and

A green leaf of language comes twisting out of her mouth.

Eiléan Ní Chuilleanáin

Merlin

I will consider the outnumbering dead:

For they are the husks of what was rich seed.

Now, should they come together to be fed,

They would outstrip the locusts' covering tide.

Arthur, Elaine, Mordred; they are all gone

Among the raftered galleries of bone.

By the long barrows of Logres they are made one,

And over their city stands the pinnacled corn.

Geoffrey Hill

Les oiseaux continuent à chanter

Abattez mes branches

sciez-moi en morceaux

les oiseaux continuent à chanter

dans mes racines

Anise Koltz

The birds will still sing

Break my branches
saw me into bits
the birds will still sing
in my roots.

Translation by John Montague

Nana

Duerme,
que en el mar, huerto perdido,
va y viene, amante, tu peine,
por los cabellos, mi vida,
de una sirenita verde.

De una verde sirenita,
que se los peina a la orilla,
mientras la orilla va y viene.

Duerme, mi amante,
porque va y viene.

Rafael Alberti

Lullaby

Sleep, my love.

On the lost orchard of the sea

Your comb plies back and forth

Through a green mermaid's hair ...

A little green mermaid

Who combs her hair by the sea

As the shore swings back and forth.

Sleep, my love.

Back and forth it swings.

Translation by Michael Smith

Fís Dheireanach Eoghain Rua Uí Shúilleabháin

Do thál bó na maidine

ceo bainne ar gach gleann

is tháinig glór cos anall

ó shleasa bána na mbeann.

Chonaic mé, mar scáileanna,

mo spailpíní fánacha,

is in ionad sleán nó rámhainn acu

bhí rós ar ghualainn chách.

Michael Hartnett

The Last Vision of Eoghan Rua Ó Súilleabháin

The cow of morning spurted

milk-mist on each glen

and the noise of feet came

from the hills' white sides.

I saw like phantoms

my fellow-workers

and instead of spades and shovels

they had roses on their shoulders.

Michael Hartnett

Vuilniszakken

Zoals ze daar 's morgens

op de stoep tegen elkaar

aan geleund warmte zoekend

in hun plastic jassen

staan te wachten, grijs,

vormeloos, vol afgedankt

leven, tegelijk broos

en weerloos. Je zou ze

weer naar binnen willen

halen, je ouders

wachtend op de bus.

Victor Vroomkoning

Rubbish Bags

The way they wait there

on the pavement in the dawn

huddled against each other

seeking warmth in plastic coats,

grey, formless, full of spurned life,

feeble and helpless. You'd like

to take them in again, your

parents waiting for the bus.

Translation by Dennis O'Driscoll

and Peter van de Kamp

Di te non scriverò

a mia madre

Di te non scriverò,

io sono tutta scritta di te.

Non c'è al di là del mio margine ombroso

pagina chiara che ti possa accogliere.

Elena Clementelli

I will not write of you

to my mother

I will not write of you,
I am your image.
There is not beyond my shady margin
any clear page that could greet you.

Translation by Catherine O'Brien

Na h-Eilthirich

A liuthad soitheach a dh'fhàg ar dùthaich
le sgiathan geala a' toirt Chanada orra.
Tha iad mar neapaigearan 'nar cuimhne
's an sàl mar dheòirean
's anns na croinn aca seòladairean a' seinn
mar eòin air gheugan.
Muir a' Mhàigh ud gu gorm a' ruith,
gealach air an oidhch', grian air an latha,
ach a' ghealach mar mheas buidhe,
mar thruinnsear air balla,
ris an tog iad an làmhan,
neo mar mhagnet airgeadach
le gathan goirte
a' sruthadh do'n chridhe.

Iain Crichton Smith

The Exiles

The many ships that left our country

with white wings for Canada.

They are like handkerchiefs in our memories

and the brine like tears

and in their masts sailors singing

like birds on branches.

That sea of May running in such blue,

a moon at night, a sun at daytime,

and the moon like a yellow fruit,

like a plate on a wall

to which they raise their hands

like a silver magnet

with piercing rays

streaming into the heart.

Iain Crichton Smith

Fotografierne

Hun standser og puster på øverste trin.
Alle de trapper, alle de år—.
Står med den kolde nøgle i hånden
og lytter efter tyve.

Snak—der er kun fotografierne,
godmodige, fremstående øjne.
Sådan ser ingen ud mere.

Endelig glider hun gennem sprækken
som et tyndt brev til sig selv.

Benny Andersen

Photographs

She stops and pauses for breath at the landing.

All those stairs, all those years—

stands with the cold key in her hand

and listens for thieves.

Nonsense—there are only photographs in there,

good-natured, prominent eyes.

No one looks like that anymore.

At last she glides through the slot

like a thin letter to herself.

Translation by Alexander Taylor

Història

Aquí és un home

Aquí és un cadàver

Aquí és una estàtua.

Joan Brossa

History

Here a man

Here a corpse

Here a statue.

Translation by Susan Schreibman

Border Lake

The farther North you travel, the colder it gets.
Take that border county of which no one speaks.
Look at the straggly length of its capital town:
the bleakness after a fair, cattle beaten home.
The only beauty nearby is a small glacial lake
sheltering between drumlin moons of mountains.
In winter it is completely frozen over, reeds
bayonet sharp, under a low, comfortless sky.
Near the middle there is a sluggish channel
where a stray current tugs to free itself.
The solitary pair of swans who haunt the lake
have found it out, and come zigzagging,
holding their breasts aloof from the jagged
edges of large pale mirrors of ice.

John Montague

First Fig

My candle burns at both ends;

    It will not last the night;

But ah, my foes, and oh, my friends—

    It gives a lovely light!

Edna St Vincent Millay

She Tells Her Love While Half Asleep

She tells her love while half asleep,
   In the dark hours,
      With half-words whispered low:
As Earth stirs in her winter sleep
   And puts out grass and flowers
      Despite the snow,
      Despite the falling snow.

Robert Graves

How dear to me the hour

How dear to me the hour when daylight dies,
    And sunbeams melt along the silent sea;
For then sweet dreams of other days arise,
    And memory breathes her vesper sigh to thee.

And, as I watch the line of light, that plays
    Along the smooth wave tow'rd the burning west,
I long to tread that golden path of rays,
    And think 'twould lead to some bright isle of rest.

Thomas Moore

Thought of Dedalus

Is this the tide coming in
  or the tide going out?
Do I keep silence
  or do I shout?

Hugh Maxton

Heraclitus

They told me, Heraclitus, they told me you were dead,

They brought me bitter news to hear and bitter tears to shed.

I wept as I remembered how often you and I

Had tired the sun with talking and sent him down the sky.

And now that thou art lying, my dear old Carian guest,

A handful of grey ashes, long, long ago at rest,

Still are thy pleasant voices, thy nightingales, awake;

For Death, he taketh all away, but them he cannot take.

William Johnson Cory

Cléithín

Ba gheall le mionsamhail
De dhealbh éigin de chuid Calder
An cachtas agat sa chistin,
Rian do bhanaltrachta ar a leathláimh leonta—
Cléithín!
Ní fhaca
Is ní dócha go bhfeicfead choíche
Cineáltacht mar é
Le ní briogadánach.
Dhoirtis grá
Is bhí an uile ní faoi bhláth.

Gabriel Rosenstock

Splint

It was like a miniature

of some sculpture by Calder,

your cactus in the kitchen.

It had signs of your nursing

on one broken limb—

A splint!

I never saw

(nor don't suppose I will)

such kindness

to a prickly thing.

You poured out love in that room

and every thing burst into bloom.

Gabriel Rosenstock

Pot Burial

He has married again. His wife
Buys ornaments and places them
On the dark sideboard. Year by year
Her vases and small jugs crowd out
The smiles of the wife who died.

Tom Paulin

Political Greatness

Nor happiness, nor majesty, nor fame,
Nor peace, nor strength, nor skill in arms or arts,
Shepherd those herds whom tyranny makes tame;
Verse echoes not one beating of their hearts,
History is but the shadow of their shame,
Art veils her glass, or from the pageant starts
As to oblivion their blind millions fleet,
Staining that Heaven with obscene imagery
Of their own likeness. What are numbers knit
By force or custom? Man who man would be,
Must rule the empire of himself; in it
Must be supreme, establishing his throne
On vanquished will, quelling the anarchy
Of hopes and fears, being himself alone.

Percy Bysshe Shelley

Sonnet VIII

The apples ripen under yellowing leaves,
And in the farm yards by the little bay
The shadows come and go amid the sheaves,
And on the long dry inland winding way:
Where, in the thinning boughs each air bereaves,
Faint sunlight's golden, and the spider weaves.
Grey are the low-laid sleepy hills, and grey
The autumn solitude of the sea day,
Where from the deep 'mid-channel, less and less
You hear along the pale east afternoon
A sound, uncertain as the silence, swoon—
The tide's sad voice ebbing towards loneliness:
And past the sands and seas' blue level line,
Ceaseless, the faint far murmur of the brine.

Thomas Caulfield Irwin

Fear

Fear passes from man to man
Unknowing,
As one leaf passes its shudder
To another.

All at once the whole tree is trembling
and there is no sign of the wind.

Charles Simic

To a Fat Lady Seen from the Train

O why do you walk through the fields in gloves,
  Missing so much and so much?
O fat white woman whom nobody loves,
Why do you walk through the fields in gloves,
When the grass is soft as the breast of doves
  And shivering-sweet to the touch?
O why do you walk through the fields in gloves,
  Missing so much and so much?

Frances Cornford

Throwing the Beads

A mother at Shannon, waving to her son

Setting out from North Kerry, flung

A rosary beads out to the tarmac

Suddenly as a lifebelt hurled from a pier.

Don't forget to say your prayers in Boston.

She saw the bright crucifix among skyscrapers,

Shielding him from harm in streets out of serials,

Comforting as a fat Irish cop in a gangster film

Rattling his baton along a railing after dark.

Seán Dunne

To My Inhaler

When the Walls of Jericho came tumbling down
the day was filled with dust and cries.
One breathless night remembering it all
from storybook pictures in Sunday School—

gaunt men with beards like washing-boards
blew trumpets till the city fell,
their ashen faces and dreadful locks,
the teacher's depiction of The Wages of Sin—

I played upon this alto of metered air
and slowly the sounds cleared
to our baby girl piping up
in her own dark world.

Gerald Dawe

au pair girl

```
 pair g
 au pair
ir girl a
u pair gi
 pair girl
au pair girl
girl au pair g
u pair girl au pa
girl au pair girl au
rl au pair girl au p
girl au pair girl au
ir girl au pair girl
u pair girl au p
au pair girl
```

Ian Hamilton Finlay

Les Silhouettes

The sea is flecked with bars of grey,
   The dull dead wind is out of tune,
   And like a withered leaf the moon
Is blown across the stormy bay.

Etched clear upon the pallid sand
   Lies the black boat: a sailor boy
   Clambers aboard in careless joy
With laughing face and gleaming hand.

And overhead the curlews cry,
   Where through the dusky upland grass
   The young brown-throated reapers pass,
Like silhouettes against the sky.

Oscar Wilde

The Distances

Driving along the unfenced road
in August dusk, the sun gone from
an empty sky, we overtook
a man walking his dog on the turf.

The parked car we passed later,
its sidelights on, a woman
shadow in the dark interior
sitting upright, motionless.

And fifty yards farther a runner
in shorts pacing steadily;
and I thought of the distances
of loneliness.

John Hewitt

Song

I wish I was where I would be

With love alone to dwell

Was I but her or she but me

Then love would all be well

I wish to send my thoughts to her

As quick as thoughts can fly

But as the wind the waters stir

The mirrors change and flye

John Clare

Anthem for Doomed Youth

What passing-bells for these who die as cattle?
    Only the monstrous anger of the guns.
    Only the stuttering rifles' rapid rattle
Can patter out their hasty orisons.
No mockeries now for them; no prayers nor bells,
    Nor any voice of mourning save the choirs,—
The shrill, demented choirs of wailing shells;
    And bugles calling for them from sad shires.

What candles may be held to speed them all?
    Not in the hands of boys, but in their eyes
Shall shine the holy glimmers of good-byes.
    The pallor of girls' brows shall be their pall;
Their flowers the tenderness of patient minds,
And each slow dusk a drawing-down of blinds.

Wilfred Owen

Above the Dock

Above the quiet dock in midnight,
Tangled in the tall mast's corded height,
Hangs the moon. What seemed so far away
Is but a child's balloon, forgotten after play.

T.E. Hulme

Proof

I would like all things to be free of me,
Never to murder the days with presupposition,
Never to feel they suffer the imposition
Of having to be this or that. How easy
It is to maim the moment
With expectation, to force it to define
Itself. Beyond all that I am, the sun
Scatters its light as though by accident.

The fox eats its own leg in the trap
To go free. As it limps through the grass
The earth itself appears to bleed.
When the morning light comes up
Who knows what suffering midnight was?
Proof is what I do not need.

Brendan Kennelly

Tilly

He travels after a winter sun,
Urging the cattle along a cold red road,
Calling to them, a voice they know,
He drives his beasts above Cabra.

The voice tells them home is warm.
They moo and make brute music with their hoofs.
He drives them with a flowering branch before him,
Smoke pluming their foreheads.

Boor, bond of the herd,
Tonight stretch full by the fire!
I bleed by the black stream
For my torn bough!

James Joyce

Two Winos

Most days you will find this pair reclining on the waste
  ground
Between Electric Street and Hemp Street, sharing a
  bottle of Drawbridge
British Wine. They stare at isolated clouds, or puffs of
  steam which leak out
From the broken pipes and vents at the back of the
  Franklin Laundry...
They converse in snarls and giggles, and they
  understand each other perfectly.

Just now they have entered the giggling phase, though
  what there is
To laugh at, who knows. Unless it was this momentary
  ray of sunlight
That glanced across their patch of crushed coke,
  broken glass and cinders;
And the bottle which had seemed half-empty until then
  is now half-full.

Ciaran Carson

Once it was the colour of saying

Once it was the colour of saying
Soaked my table the uglier side of a hill
With a capsized field where a school sat still
And a black and white patch of girls grew playing;
The gentle seaslides of saying I must undo
That all the charmingly drowned arise to cockcrow and kill.
When I whistled with mitching boys through a reservoir park
Where at night we stoned the cold and cuckoo
Lovers in the dirt of their leafy beds,
The shade of their trees was a word of many shades
And a lamp of lightning for the poor in the dark;
Now my saying shall be my undoing,
And every stone I wind off like a reel.

Dylan Thomas

Piazza di Spagna, Early Morning

I can't forget

How she stood at the top of that long marble stair

Amazed, and then with a sleepy pirouette

Went dancing slowly down to the fountain-quieted square;

Nothing upon her face

But some impersonal loneliness,—not then a girl,

But as it were a reverie of the place,

A called-for falling glide and whirl;

As when a leaf, petal, or thin chip

Is drawn to the falls of a pool and, circling a moment above it,

Rides on over the lip—

Perfectly beautiful, perfectly ignorant of it.

Richard Wilbur

Body

I'll wear it out perhaps
To a suit of wrinkle, a skin
Too large
With the soul shrinking;

The will gone out of it,
Yet all the daily rent to pay;
Flesh that cannot last,
Soul that never got under way:

Too much houseroom now;
Tomorrow none;
But paying either way
For journey done, for journey not begun.

Padraic Fallon

Work Without Hope

All Nature seems at work. Slugs leave their lair—
The bees are stirring—birds are on the wing—
And Winter, slumbering in the open air,
Wears on his smiling face a dream of Spring!
And I, the while, the sole unbusy thing,
Nor honey make, nor pair, nor build, nor sing.

Yet well I ken the banks where amaranths blow,
Have traced the fount whence streams of nectar flow.
Bloom, O ye amaranths! bloom for whom he may,
For me ye bloom not! Glide, rich streams, away!
With lips unbrighten'd, wreathless brow, I stroll:
And would you learn the spells that drowse my soul?
Work without hope draws nectar in a sieve,
And hope without an object cannot live.

Samuel Taylor Coleridge

The Demolition

They have lived in each other so long
there is little to do there.
They have taken to patching the floor
while the roof tears.

The rot in her feeds on his woodwork.
He batters her cellar.
He camps in the ruins of her carpet.
She cries on his stairs.

Anne Stevenson

October

O leafy yellowness you create for me

A world that was and now is poised above time,

I do not need to puzzle out Eternity

As I walk this arboreal street on the edge of a town.

The breeze too, even the temperature

And pattern of movement is precisely the same

As broke my heart for youth passing. Now I am sure

Of something. Something will be mine wherever I am.

I want to throw myself on the public street without caring

For anything but the prayering that the earth offers.

It is October over all my life and the light is staring

As it caught me once in a plantation by the fox coverts.

A man is ploughing ground for winter wheat

And my nineteen years weigh heavily on my feet.

Patrick Kavanagh

Requiem

Under the wide and starry sky,
Dig the grave and let me lie.
Glad did I live and gladly die,
   And I laid me down with a will.

This be the verse you grave for me:
Here he lies where he longed to be;
Home is the sailor, home from sea,
   And the hunter home from the hill.

Robert Louis Stevenson

3 A.M.

I'll give him a minute longer
before I break the news.
Another minute of innocence and rest.
He is in the thicket of dreams
he will still be struggling with
as he stirs himself to take my call
wondering who in Christ's name
this could be.
       One more minute, then,
to let him sleep through what
he's just about to wake to.

Dennis O'Driscoll

Taxman

Seven scythes leaned at the wall.

Beard upon golden beard

The last barley load

Swayed through the yard.

The girls uncorked the ale.

Fiddle and feet moved together.

Then between stubble and heather

A horseman rode.

George Mackay Brown

The Bed

The pulsing stops where time has been,
    The garden is snow-bound,
The branches weighed down and the paths filled in,
    Drifts quilt the ground.

We lie soft-caught, still now it's done,
    Loose-twined across the bed
Like wrestling statues; but it still goes on
    Inside my head.

Thom Gunn

My Mother

My mother's smell is sweet or sour and moist

Like the soft red cover of the apple.

She sits among her boxes, lace and tins,

And notices the smallest of all breezes,

As if she were a tree upon the mountain

Growing away with no problem at all.

Her swan's head quivers like a light-bulb:

Does she breed in perfect peace, a light sleep,

Or smothered like a clock whose alarm

Is unendurable, whose featureless

Straight face is never wrong?

No one knows what goes on inside a clock.

Medbh McGuckian

The Five Senses

The steady hiss of the tilly,
The groaning rain barrel;

Boiled bollan,
Baled hay;

The fossil on the stone
Where the soap sits;

Tall moon-white daisies
On the bank, shaking,

And sea salt
In the sea mist.

Dermot Healy

The Death of Irish

The tide gone out for good,
Thirty-one words for seaweed
Whiten on the foreshore.

Aidan Mathews

Variations on a Theme of Chardin

like wanting to photograph light itself:

not as it falls across an upholstered chair,
a book, a dusty window,

but peeled intact off surfaces
as a child floats a faded stamp
tenderly off its scrap of blue paper

or as you walk through lone
nectarine evenings

the print of his hand still watermarks your spine

Ruth Valentine

Sonnet XX (On his Blindness)

When I consider how my light is spent,
  Ere half my days, in this dark world and wide,
  And that one talent which is death to hide
  Lodged with me useless, though my soul more bent
To serve therewith my Maker, and present
  My true account, lest he returning chide,
  'Doth God exact day-labour, light denied?'
  I fondly ask. But patience, to prevent
That murmur, soon replies, 'God doth not need
  Either man's work or his own gifts; who best
  Bear his mild yoke, they serve him best. His state
Is kingly. Thousands at his bidding speed,
  And post o'er land and ocean without rest;
  They also serve who only stand and wait.'

John Milton

Frozen Rain

I slow down the waterfall to a chandelier,
Filaments of daylight, bones fleshed out by ice
That recuperate in their bandages of glass
And, where the lake behaves like a spirit-level,
I save pockets of air for the otter to breathe.

I magnify each individual blade of grass
With frozen rain, a crop of icicles and twigs,
Fingers and thumbs that beckon towards the thaw
And melt to the marrow between lip and tongue
While the wind strikes the branches like a celeste.

Michael Longley

Vengeance

I am a child of the poor.

For me there will have to be

Tinfoil: the pink light
-ning pale aquamarine
Morning sea-splashed

Soil dream against

The grave night gale.

Padraic Fiacc

Old Age

The seas are quiet when the winds give o'er;
So calm are we when passions are no more.
For then we know how vain it was to boast
Of fleeting things, so certain to be lost.
Clouds of affection from our younger eyes
Conceal that emptiness which age descries.

The soul's dark cottage, battered and decayed,
Lets in new light through chinks that Time has made:
Stronger by weakness, wiser men become
As they draw near to their eternal home.
Leaving the old, both worlds at once they view
That stand upon the threshold of the new.

Edmund Waller

Dolor

I have known the inexorable sadness of pencils,

Neat in their boxes, dolor of pad and paper-weight,

All the misery of manilla folders and mucilage,

Desolation in immaculate public places,

Lonely reception room, lavatory, switchboard,

The unalterable pathos of basin and pitcher,

Ritual of multigraph, paper-clip, comma,

Endless duplication of lives and objects.

And I have seen dust from the walls of institutions,

Finer than flour, alive, more dangerous than silica,

Sift, almost invisible, through long afternoons of tedium,

Dropping a fine film on nails and delicate eyebrows,

Glazing the pale hair, the duplicate grey standard faces.

Theodore Roethke

Post-script: for Gweno

If I should go away,

Beloved, do not say

'He has forgotten me'.

For you abide,

A singing rib within my dreaming side;

You always stay.

And in the mad tormented valley

Where blood and hunger rally

And Death the wild beast is uncaught, untamed,

Our soul withstands the terror

And has its quiet honour

Among the glittering stars your voices named.

Alun Lewis

Asleep in the City

The church steeple fingers the sky,

The cold air glints like frost against the stars

And the moon's casual indifferent face

Simply there in the broken sky,

Bird-high above the small terraced houses

Where people dream in the hard night

Of their own private suns:

Red things beating still beneath the packed snow.

Michael Smith

Retreat

Day peters out. Darkness wells up
  From wheelrut, culvert, vacant drain;
But still a rooster glints with life,
  High on a church's weather-vane;
The sun flings Mycenaean gold
  Against a neighbor's window-pane.

Anthony Hecht

Sa Chaife

daoine

ag féachaint ar

dhaoine

ag féachaint ar

dhaoine

ag féachaint

is féachfaidh

go mbeidh

duilleoga

deireanacha

na gcupán tae

le feiscint

Liam Ó Muirthile

In the Café

people stare

at people staring

at other people

staring

and all will go on staring

until

all the lonely tea-leaves

of all their tea-cups

show

Translation by Eoghan Ó hAnluain

Under the Stairs

Look in the dark alcove under the stairs:
a paintbrush steeped in turpentine, its hairs

softening for use; rat-poison in a jar;
bent spoons for prising lids; a spare fire-bar;

the shaft of a broom; a tyre; assorted nails;
a store of candles for when the light fails.

Frank Ormsby

Buffalo Bill's

defunct

     who used to

     ride a watersmooth-silver

               stallion

and break onetwothreefourfive pigeonsjustlikethat

                     Jesus

he was a handsome man

          and what i want to know is

how do you like your blueeyed boy

Mister Death

e.e. cummings

Mrs Sweeney

I cast my song on the water.

The sky stirs,

clouds are driven under the trailing willow.

I cast my song on the water.

The sky in your hungry eye, you drop

to meet the cloud's image.

Your eye most nights is sparrowhawk.

So strike. Flip me over. Pin

my wings with your talons.

Pluck, then, my breast feathers

to the creamy skin over my heart.

Flash of beak as you stoop to pierce.

Paula Meehan

The Tired Scribe

from the Irish

My hand has a pain from writing,
Not steady the sharp tool of my craft
Its slender beak spews bright ink—
A beetle-dark shining draught.

Streams of wisdom of white God
From my fair-brown, fine hand sally,
On the page they splash their flood
In ink of the green-skinned holly.

My little dribbly pen stretches
Across the great white paper plain,
Insatiable for splendid riches—
That is why my hand has pain!

Brian O'Nolan

Gare du Midi

A nondescript express in from the South,
Crowds round the ticket barrier, a face
To welcome which the mayor has not contrived
Bugles or braid: something about the mouth
Distracts the stray look with alarm and pity.
Snow is falling. Clutching a little case,
He walks out briskly to infect a city
Whose terrible future may have just arrived.

W.H. Auden

Love and Friendship

Love is like the wild rose-briar,
Friendship like the holly tree—
The holly is dark when the rose-briar blooms
But which will bloom most constantly?

The wild rose-briar is sweet in spring,
Its summer blossoms scent the air;
Yet wait till winter comes again
And who will call the wild-briar fair?

Then scorn the silly rose-wreath now
And deck thee with the holly's sheen,
That when December blights thy brow
He still may leave thy garland green.

Emily Brontë

Their Laughter

Anything can happen here, though it's dinner

and everybody seems calm, my father

winding himself down with jokes and sighs,

my mother smiling and eating. I shuffle them like cards

until something turns up, a house full of weapons

and strangers, a garden mined with quiet.

In love with death, I give them each

two minutes to live and leave the table.

I set the charge and wait for it, first

the explosion, then the indulgent shrapnel

piercing the hall and landing, raining on me

all the way up the stairs.

Peter Sirr

There are established personal places
that receive our lives' heat
and adapt in their mass, like stone.

These absorb in their changes
the radiance of change in us,
and give it back

to the darkness of our understanding,
directionless
into the returning cold.

Thomas Kinsella

The Bright Field

I have seen the sun break through
to illuminate a small field
for a while, and gone my way
and forgotten it. But that was the pearl
of great price, the one field that had
the treasure in it. I realize now
that I must give all that I have
to possess it. Life is not hurrying

on to a receding future, nor hankering after
an imagined past. It is the turning
aside like Moses to the miracle
of the lit bush, to a brightness
that seemed as transitory as your youth
once, but is the eternity that awaits you.

R.S. *Thomas*

Biographical notes

Rafael Alberti (1902–) was born in Puerto de Santa María, near Cádiz. He fought on the Republican side in the Spanish Civil War. Later he lived in exile in Paris, Buenos Aires and Rome. He returned to Spain in 1977 and briefly again took up active politics, winning a seat in the Cortes as a communist.

William Allingham (1824–89) was born in Ballyshannon, Co. Donegal. He became a customs officer in the town. His first volume of poetry was published in 1850. Many of his poems were sold widely in Ireland as halfpenny broadsheets. His most ambitious work is *Laurence Bloomfield in Ireland* (1864). In 1870 Allingham retired to London; he died in Hampstead.

Benny Andersen (1929–) was born in Copenhagen. After an apprenticeship in an advertising agency, he spent most of the 1950s as a travelling pianist, playing in bars and hotels all over Scandinavia. Since 1962 he has been a full-time author, songwriter and composer.

W.H. Auden (1907–73) was born in York and was brought up in Birmingham. He studied at Christ Church, Oxford. In the 1930s he collaborated on various literary projects with Louis MacNeice (a travel book) and Christopher Isherwood (verse plays). In 1939 Auden left England and settled in the United States, taking up American citizenship in 1946. His collections include *Look, Stranger!* (1936), *The Shield of Achilles* (1955) and *City Without Walls* (1969). From 1956 to 1960 he was Professor of Poetry at Oxford.

Samuel Beckett (1906–89) was born in Foxrock, Co. Dublin and studied at Portora Royal School, Enniskillen and at Trinity College, Dublin. In the 1930s he settled in Paris. *Waiting for Godot* was the work that made his name. He is best known as a dramatist and a novelist, but he wrote poems throughout his career. He was awarded the Nobel Prize for Literature in 1969.

Brendan Behan (1923–64) was born in Dublin. He joined the IRA aged fourteen. In 1939 he was arrested in Liverpool for carrying explosives and was sentenced to three years in Borstal, an experience that inspired the best-selling *Borstal Boy* (1958). A later prison sentence gave rise to his play *The Quare Fellow* (1954). Behan learned Irish while in jail and began to write poetry; indeed, his first published work was in the Irish language.

147

Elizabeth Bishop (1911–79) was born in Worcester, Massachusetts, but was raised by her maternal grandparents in Nova Scotia. She began writing poems at Vassar College, where she met Marianne Moore. All her life she was an enthusiastic traveller and she lived in Brazil for nearly twenty years. Her collection *North and South* (1946) made her reputation. Her last book was *Geography III* (1976).

William Blake (1757–1827) was born in London. He had no formal education, except in art. At fourteen he was apprenticed to an engraver. In 1782 he married Catherine Boucher, the daughter of a market gardener, and taught her to read and write. Blake had to struggle as an artist and it was not until the end of his life that he achieved recognition. He printed most of his own books from copper plates, on which he engraved drawings and the texts of his poems. His best-known books are *Songs of Innocence* (1789) and *Songs of Experience* (1794).

Louise Bogan (1897–1970) was born in Livermore Falls, Maine and studied at Boston University. For nearly forty years she was poetry editor of *The New Yorker* and she taught at several American universities. Her best-known book is *The Blue Estuaries, Poems 1923–1968*.

Eavan Boland (1944–) was born in Dublin and was educated in London, New York, and at Trinity College, Dublin. Her collections include *The War Horse* (1975), *In Her Own Image* (1980), *The Journey* (1987) and *In a Time of Violence* (1994).

Anne Bradstreet (1612–72), *née* Bradley, was born in Northampton. At the age of sixteen she married Simon Bradstreet and, two years later, they sailed to America with the Puritan emigration. They helped to found the Massachusetts Bay Colony, of which her father and husband became governors. Besides raising eight children, she was the first American woman to devote herself to writing. 'To My Dear and Loving Husband' appeared six years after her death.

Rory Brennan (1945–), born in Westport, Co. Mayo, grew up in Dublin. After graduating from Trinity College, he worked in education and broadcasting. From 1982 to 1988 he was the administrator of Poetry Ireland. Many of his poems were written on the Greek island of Paros. His collections are *The Sea on Fire* (1979) and *The Walking Wounded* (1985).

Joseph Brodsky (1940–) was born in Leningrad. He was already writing poetry at fifteen when he left school to take up manual labour. In 1964 he was sentenced to five years' hard labour in an Arctic work camp, for 'social parasitism'. The sentence was commuted in 1965 as a result of international protest. In 1972 Brodsky became an involuntary exile from the Soviet Union and settled in the United States. He received the Nobel Prize for Literature in

1987. His books include *A Part of Speech* (1980), *To Urania* (1988) and *Watermark* (1992).

Anne Brontë (1820–49) was born in Thornton, Yorkshire and grew up at Haworth Parsonage, the youngest of a remarkably gifted family. Her novel *Agnes Grey* (1847) presents a fictionalized account of her experiences as a governess. A second novel, *The Tenant of Wildfell Hall*, was published a year before her death. She died and is buried in Scarborough. 'Farewell' was written in memory of William Weightman, a curate of Haworth, who died in his twenties.

Emily Brontë (1818–48) was born in Thornton, Yorkshire. As a child, she wrote of an imaginary world, in the *Gondal* stories. Her poems were published pseudonymously with those of her sisters in *Poems, by Currer, Ellis and Acton Bell* (1846). In 1847 her novel, *Wuthering Heights,* was published as a set with her sister Anne's *Agnes Grey.*

Joan Brossa (1919–) was born in Barcelona. He is a poet and playwright and writes exclusively in his native Catalan. In 1948 Brossa was one of the founders of the Vanguardia, an artistic movement that included Joan Miró and which favoured an integrated concept of the arts.

George Mackay Brown (1921–) was born in Stromness in the Orkney Islands. He studied at Edinburgh University. His first book was published in 1954 and, since then, he has written plays, novels (including *Beside the Ocean of Time*), collections of short stories, essays and children's books, as well as numerous poetry collections. His *Portrait of Orkney* is an introduction to the islands that have always been his home.

Elizabeth Barrett Browning (1806–61) was born in County Durham and began writing poetry as a child. In 1845 she met Robert Browning. They married, secretly and against her father's will, and fled to Italy. From 1847 until her death, she lived in Florence and was never reconciled with her family. *Sonnets from the Portuguese* (1850) comprises 44 love poems, written in secret about the time of her marriage.

Ciaran Carson (1948–) was born in Belfast and studied at Queen's University. He has worked as a teacher, but is now the traditional arts officer of the Arts Council of Northern Ireland. His collections are *The New Estate* (1976), *The Irish for No* (1987), *Belfast Confetti* (1989) and *First Language* (1993). He is also the author of *The Pocket Guide to Irish Traditional Music* (1986).

John Clare (1793–1864) was born in Helpstone, Northamptonshire. His father was a labourer, and Clare, too, worked on the land. His first book, *Poems Descriptive of Rural Life and Scenery*, was published in 1820. He went to

149

London and there met Coleridge and Hazlitt. His most famous work, *The Shepherd's Calendar*, appeared in 1827. Clare lived an impoverished life, his health deteriorated, and in 1837 delusions and mental disorder forced his removal to an asylum.

Austin Clarke (1896–1974) was born in Dublin and studied at the National University. He spent a great deal of the 1920s and 30s in England, supporting his poetry with literary journalism. The first phase of Clarke's poetic career was completed with the publication of *Night and Morning* in 1938. Seventeen years later, with *Ancient Lights*, he entered a new period of poetic activity, culminating in his *Collected Poems* of 1974.

Elena Clementelli (1923–) was born in Rome and studied Spanish literature at Rome University. Her first collection of poetry was published in 1957 and since then she has won several literary awards. She lives in Rome, where she worked until her retirement at the Italo-Latin American Institute.

Samuel Taylor Coleridge (1772–1834) was born in Ottery St Mary, Devon and studied at Cambridge University. In his earliest years he was radical in politics and religion and during this time wrote his best-known poetry. *Lyrical Ballads*, which contains 'The Rime of the Ancient Mariner', was published in 1798. Coleridge turned increasingly to philosophy and religion in his later years, which were troubled by personal difficulties and opium addiction. 'Work Without Hope' is characteristic of a number of poems he wrote in the last decade of his life as his spirits revived.

Frances Cornford (1886–1960), a grand-daughter of Charles Darwin, was born and lived in Cambridge, where her parents were university lecturers. She published her first book of poetry in 1909. Later volumes include *Spring Morning* (1915), *Autumn Midnight* (1923) and *On a Calm Shore* (1960).

William Johnson Cory (1823–92) was born in Torrington, Devon and studied at Eton and Cambridge. He taught at Eton for more than a quarter of a century and, in 1863, wrote the 'Eton Boating Song'. *Ionica*, a collection of his lyrics, was published anonymously in 1858.

Anthony Cronin (1925–) was born in Enniscorthy, Co. Wexford and studied at University College, Dublin. He has had a varied career as poet, novelist, essayist, critic, journalist, broadcaster and cultural advisor. His books include *The Life of Riley* (1964), *Dead as Doornails* (1976), *The End of the Modern World* (1989) and *No Laughing Matter: The Life and Times of Flann O'Brien* (1989). His biography of Samuel Beckett is in preparation.

e.e. cummings (1894–1962) was born in Cambridge, Massachusetts. After graduating from Harvard University, he served in an ambulance unit in the

Great War. Suspected of being a spy, he was interned in a French detention camp for three months—an experience he chronicled in *The Enormous Room* (1922). His first collection of poetry, *Tulips and Chimneys*, appeared in 1923. Besides his prolific poetic output, cummings painted and wrote plays. *Eimi* (1933) is a book about his travels in Russia.

Michael Davitt (1950–) was born in Cork. As a student at University College, Cork in 1970, he founded the poetry journal *Innti*, which became a major forum for the flowering of Irish-language poetry. His books include *Bligeárd Sráide* (1983) and *Selected Poems/Rogha Dánta 1968–1984* (1987).

Gerald Dawe (1952–) was born in Belfast and studied at Orangefield Boys' School, the University of Ulster and University College, Galway. His collections of poetry include *Sheltering Places* (1978), *The Lundys Letter* (1985) and *Sunday School* (1991). He is the editor of the arts review *Krino* and teaches at Trinity College, Dublin.

Seamus Deane (1940–) was born in Derry and studied at Queen's University, Belfast and Cambridge University. His publications include *Gradual Wars* (1972), *Rumours* (1977), *History Lessons* (1983), *Celtic Revivals* (1985) and *The French Enlightenment and Revolution in England 1789–1832* (1988). He was general editor of *The Field Day Anthology of Irish Writing* (1991) and is Professor of Irish Studies at the University of Notre Dame, Indiana.

Denis Devlin (1908–59) was born in Greenock, Scotland, attended Belvedere College and University College, Dublin, and entered the Irish diplomatic service in 1935. He served in New York, Washington, London and Turkey and, on his death, was Ambassador to Italy. Although he published only two collections in his lifetime, he had an international reputation. His *Collected Poems*, edited by J.C.C. Mays, was published in 1989.

Emily Dickinson (1830–86) led a life which, outwardly, was almost entirely uneventful. She was born, lived and died in the same house in Amherst, Massachusetts, and from the age of twenty-three spent her life in self-imposed seclusion, seeing nobody outside her immediate family. She left behind 1775 poems; only seven of them were published, anonymously, during her lifetime.

John Donne (*c.*1572–1631) was born in London of Catholic parents (his mother was a descendant of Thomas More). After studying at Oxford, Cambridge and the Inns of Court, he travelled in Europe on various ambassadorial ventures. He became a Protestant, was ordained in 1615 and eventually was appointed Dean of St Paul's. Donne is equally well known as a love poet and for his 'Divine poems'.

Seán Dunne (1956–) was born in Waterford and studied at University College,

Cork. His two collections of poetry are *Against the Storm* (1985) and *The Sheltered Nest* (1992). He has written a memoir, *In My Father's House* (1991), and edited *The Cork Anthology* (1993); his most recent book is *The Road to Silence* (1994). He is literary editor of *The Cork Examiner*.

T.S. Eliot (1888–1965) was born in St Louis, Missouri. He studied at Harvard, the Sorbonne, Oxford and Marburg. His first collection of poems was published in 1917, but it was *The Waste Land* (1922) that made him famous. Eliot worked as a bank clerk until he joined the publishers Faber and Faber in 1925. Besides being one of the twentieth century's most influential poets, he also wrote verse drama and literary criticism. He was awarded the Nobel Prize for Literature in 1948.

Padraic Fallon (1905–74) was born in Athenry, Co. Galway and studied in Ballinasloe and Roscrea. At the age of eighteen he joined the Customs and Excise Service in Dublin and at this time came under the influence of George Russell (AE). In 1939 he took up a post in Wexford and stayed there until 1963. He wrote plays for radio, including the verse drama *The Vision of Mac Conglinne* (1953), and two stage plays. He had an aversion to publication and refused to collect his poems until shortly before his death.

Padraic Fiacc (1924–) was born Patrick Joseph O'Connor in the Markets area of Belfast. His father emigrated to the United States and was followed in 1929 by his wife and their three sons; the family settled in Manhattan where Fiacc attended a seminary. He abandoned his studies and in 1946 returned to Belfast, where he still lives. *Ruined Pages: Selected Poems of Padraic Fiacc* was published in 1994.

Ian Hamilton Finlay (1925–) was born in Nassau, Bahamas, but has lived most of his life in the north of Scotland. He is a pioneer of the concrete poetry movement and has produced paper sculpture poems and large poem-constructions in glass and concrete. He is a significant figure in landscape art, and has worked in Germany, France and the United States.

Robert Frost (1874–1963) was born in San Francisco, but on his father's death, ten years later, was brought to New England. In 1912 he went with his wife and children to England, and his first book, *A Boy's Will*, was published there the next year. *North of Boston* came out in 1914. Frost spent most of his later life on a farm in New Hampshire. He received many honours and became America's unofficial poet laureate.

Oliver St John Gogarty (1878–1957) was born in Dublin and studied medicine at Trinity College, Dublin. He became a successful nose and throat surgeon, was a renowned conversationalist, served in Seanad Éireann from 1922 to 1936, and is the prototype for Buck Mulligan in Joyce's *Ulysses*. His most famous work is the autobiographical *As I Was Going Down Sackville Street* (1937), but he wrote many volumes of poetry. Gogarty left Ireland in 1939 and lived in New York for the rest of his life.

Robert Graves (1895–1985) was born in Wimbledon and studied at Charterhouse, from where he went straight to the trenches on the Western Front. He was wounded at the Somme and suffered from shell-shock for many years. The success of the autobiographical *Goodbye to All That* (1929) enabled him to emigrate to Majorca. Graves was Professor of Poetry at Oxford from 1961 to 1966. He wrote historical novels (*I, Claudius* is the best known) and mythology (*The White Goddess*), but poetry was always primary.

Thom Gunn (1929–) was born in Gravesend, Kent and studied at Trinity College, Cambridge. His first book, *Fighting Terms*, was published in 1954 while he was still an undergraduate. He moved to California and now teaches at the University of California, Berkeley. His books include *My Sad Captains* (1961), *Moly* (1970), *Jack Straw's Castle* (1976) and *The Man with Night Sweats* (1992). His *Collected Poems* was published in 1993.

Thomas Hardy (1840–1928) was born in Upper Bockhampton, Dorset, the son of a stonemason. He was apprenticed to a Dorchester architect and retained throughout his long life an interest in stonework and architecture. Hardy began writing in London in 1862. His novels made him known internationally, yet, although he did not begin publishing poetry until 1898, he always regarded himself principally as a poet.

Michael Hartnett (1941–) was born in Croom, Co. Limerick. His collections include *A Farewell to English* (1975), *A Necklace of Wrens* (1987), *Poems to Younger Women* (1988), *The Killing of Dreams* (1992) and *Selected and New Poems* (1994). He has translated extensively from the Irish, particularly from the seventeenth-century poets Dáibhí Ó Bruadair and Haicéad.

Dermot Healy (1947–) was born in Finea, Co. Westmeath. He has written a collection of stories, *Banished Misfortune* (1982), and two novels, *Fighting with Shadows* (1984) and *A Goat's Song* (1994). His first collection of poems, *The Ballyconnell Colours*, was published in 1992. He is the editor of the community arts journal *Force 10*.

Seamus Heaney (1939–) was born in Mossbawn, Co. Derry and studied at Queen's University, Belfast. Since his first collection, *Death of a Naturalist* (1966), he has written nine books of poetry, two of prose (*Preoccupations* [1980] and *The Government of the Tongue* [1988]), and *The Cure at Troy*, a version of Sophocles' *Philoctetes*. He was Professor of Poetry at Oxford from 1989 to 1994 and is Boylston Professor of Rhetoric at Harvard University.

Anthony Hecht (1923–) was born in New York. He studied at Bard College and Columbia University. His first book of poems, *A Summoning of Stones*, was published in 1954. His other collections include *The Hard Hours* (1967), *The Venetian Vespers* (1979) and *The Transparent Man* (1991). He has taught at a number of universities, including Georgetown University, Washington.

John Hewitt (1907–87) was born in Belfast and studied at Queen's University. For more than twenty-five years he worked in the Belfast Museum and Art Gallery. In 1957 he became director of the art gallery and museum in Coventry, a position he held until he returned to Belfast in 1972. His books include *No Rebel Word* (1948), *Out of My Time* (1974), *Time Enough* (1976) and *The Rain Dance* (1978).

F.R. Higgins (1896–1941) was born in Foxford, Co. Mayo and grew up in County Meath. He was a pioneer of the labour movement, founded the first women's magazine in Ireland and, in 1935, was made a director of the Abbey Theatre, later becoming its business manager. His collections include *The Dark Breed* (1927), *Arable Holdings* (1933) and *The Gap of Brightness* (1940).

Geoffrey Hill (1932–) was born in Bromsgrove, Worcestershire and studied at Keble College, Oxford. For many years he taught at the University of Leeds and, later, at Cambridge University. His books include *King Log* (1968), *Mercian Hymns* (1971) and *The Mystery of the Charity of Charles Péguy* (1983). His version of Ibsen's *Brand* was produced in 1978.

Gerard Manley Hopkins (1844–89) was born in Stratford, Essex. He studied at Oxford and entered the Catholic Church in 1866. Two years later he became a Jesuit and, after he was ordained, served for a year as a priest in a slum district of Liverpool. In 1884 he was appointed Professor of Classics at University College, Dublin. Hopkins did not allow his poetry to be published during his lifetime; *Poems*, edited by his friend Robert Bridges, came out in 1918.

T.E. Hulme (1883–1917) was born in Endon, Staffordshire and studied at St John's College, Cambridge. In 1908 he formed the Poets' Club in London and it was there that he expounded his theory of 'the image' in poetry. Later his interest turned mainly to philosophy and he translated works by Henri Bergson. He was killed in action in the Great War.

Thomas Caulfield Irwin (1823–92) was born in Warrenpoint, Co. Down. In 1848 he began to write for magazines, and eventually became a regular contributor to *The Nation* and *The Dublin University Magazine*. Irwin translated several classical and contemporary European writers. His *Sonnets on the Poetry and Problems of Life* was published in 1881.

Randall Jarrell (1914–65) was born in Nashville, Tennessee and studied at Vanderbilt University. During World War II he served in the US army air corps. Later he taught at various universities. His collections include *The Seven-League Crutches* (1951) and *The Woman at the Washington Zoo* (1960). He also wrote a novel, *Pictures from an Institution* (1954), literary criticism and a book of essays, *A Sad Heart at the Supermarket* (1962).

James Joyce (1882–1941) was born in Dublin and studied at Belvedere College and the National University. In 1904 he met Nora Barnacle and they left Dublin for Zürich. Later they moved to Trieste, where Joyce taught English. They lived in Paris from 1920 until 1940, when they returned, with their children, to Zürich. Joyce's works—*Dubliners* (1914), *A Portrait of the Artist as a Young Man* (1916), *Ulysses* (1922) and *Finnegans Wake* (1939)—made him one of the most admired writers of his age. His poems were published in *Chamber Music* (1907) and *Pomes Penyeach* (1927).

Patrick Kavanagh (1905–67) was born in Iniskeen, Co. Monaghan. He worked on his father's small farm and, for a time, as a cobbler. His early books were *Ploughman and Other Poems* (1936) and the autobiographical *The Green Fool* (1938) and *Tarry Flynn* (1948). In 1939 he moved to Dublin and supported himself as a literary journalist. His major poem, *The Great Hunger*, was published in 1942, and his *Collected Poems* in 1964.

Brendan Kennelly (1936–) was born in Ballylongford, Co. Kerry and studied at Trinity College, Dublin and at the University of Leeds. His first collection, *Getting Up Early*, was published in 1966. He has since written over twenty books, including *Cromwell* (1987) and *A Time for Voices: Selected Poems 1960–1990* (1990), and has edited *The Penguin Book of Irish Verse* (1970). He is Professor of Modern Literature at Trinity College, Dublin.

Thomas Kettle (1880–1916) was born in north County Dublin, the son of one of the founders of the Land League. He practised law until his appointment as Professor of National Economy at the new National University in Dublin in 1909. From 1906 to 1910 he was MP for East Tyrone. He served with the Dublin Fusiliers in the Great War and was killed at the Somme. 'To My Daughter Betty' was written four days before his death.

Henry King (1592–1669), whose father became Bishop of London, studied at Christ Church, Oxford. John Donne and Ben Jonson were close friends. He was appointed Bishop of Chichester in 1642, was expelled during the English Civil War, but was restored to his see in 1660. King's most celebrated poem, 'The Exequy', concerns the death of his young wife, Anne Berkeley, in 1624.

Thomas Kinsella (1928–) was born in Dublin and studied at University College. He served in the Department of Finance before taking up a post at the

University of Southern Illinois and subsequently at Temple University, Philadelphia. He was a director of the Dolmen Press and the founder of the Peppercanister Press. His collections include *Downstream* (1962), *Nightwalker and Other Poems* (1968), *Notes from the Land of the Dead* (1972) and *From Centre City* (1994), as well as a translation of the Irish prose epic *Táin Bó Cuailgne* (1969).

Anise Koltz (1928–) was born in Luxembourg-Eich. In 1963 she founded the 'Journées de Mondorf', an international gathering of writers. She writes in French and German and is the author of children's stories. She is a member of the Académie Mallarmé in Paris and lives in Luxembourg.

Philip Larkin (1922–85) was born in Coventry and studied at St John's College, Oxford. He wrote two novels, worked as a university librarian in Leicester, Belfast and Hull, and for many years wrote jazz criticism. Larkin wrote sparingly, publishing only four collections during his life, including *The Whitsun Weddings* (1964) and *High Windows* (1974). His *Collected Poems*, including work he had not seen fit to publish, came out posthumously in 1988.

Francis Ledwidge (1891–1917) was born in Slane, Co. Meath, the son of an evicted tenant. He left school when he was twelve and worked as a farm labourer. Ledwidge joined the Royal Inniskilling Fusiliers in 1914, to fight 'for the fields along the Boyne, for the birds and the blue skies over them'. He was killed in action in Flanders. Most of his poetry is contained in *Songs of the Fields* (1916) and *Songs of the Peace* (1917).

Alun Lewis (1915–44) was born in Aberdare, Wales, on of a schoolmaster. He studied at University College, Aberystwyth and then joined the army. In 1942 he went to India as a lieutenant in the South Wales Borderers. He died in Arakan, Burma. His two collections are *Raiders' Dawn* (1942) and the posthumous *Ha! Ha! Among the Trumpets* (1945).

Liz Lochhead (1947–) was born in Motherwell, Scotland. She trained as a painter for eight years. Since the early 1980s she has worked increasingly in the theatre and has written many plays. Her collections include *Dreaming Frankenstein and Collected Poems* (1984), *True Confessions and New Clichés* (1985) and *Bagpipe Muzak* (1991).

Michael Longley (1939–) was born in Belfast and studied at The Royal Belfast Academical Institution and at Trinity College, Dublin. He was a schoolteacher for seven years and then worked for the Arts Council of Northern Ireland. His collections include *No Continuing City* (1969), *Man Lying on a Wall* (1976), *The Echo Gate* (1979) and *Gorse Fires* (1991).

Louis MacNeice (1907–63) was born in Belfast, raised in Carrickfergus, Co.

Antrim and studied at Merton College, Oxford. He taught Classics at Birmingham University and at Bedford College, London, but in 1941 joined the BBC as a writer and producer. His books include *Autumn Journal* (1939), *Autumn Sequel* (1954), *Visitations* (1957) and *Solstices* (1961).

Derek Mahon (1941–) was born in Belfast and studied at Trinity College, Dublin. His collections include *Night Crossing* (1968), *Courtyards in Delft* (1981), *The Hunt by Night* (1982) and *Antarctica* (1985). Among his many translations are poems by Gérard de Nerval and Philippe Jaccottet, plays by Molière and Racine, and a version of *The Bacchae* of Euripides.

Osip Mandelstam (1891–1938), born in Warsaw, grew up in St Petersburg. His collections are *Kamen* (1913), *Tristia* (1922) and *Poems* (1928). In 1934 he wrote a bitter epigram about Stalin, for which he was expelled to the Urals. In 1937 the term of exile ended and he and his wife, Nadezhda, returned to Moscow, but he was rearrested in May 1938 and is said to have died in Siberia, on the way to a concentration camp.

Aidan Mathews (1956–) was born in Dublin and studied at both University College and Trinity College there. He held a writing fellowship at Stanford University, California from 1981 to 1983 and has worked as a producer for RTÉ. His writings include plays (*Exit/Entrance* and *The Diamond Body*) and fiction (*Muesli at Midnight* and *Lipstick on the Host*), as well as his two books of poetry, *Windfalls* (1977) and *Minding Ruth* (1983).

Hugh Maxton (1947–) was born outside Aughrim, Co. Wicklow and studied at Trinity College, Dublin. He has translated the work of two Hungarian poets, Agnes Nemes Nagy and Endre Ady. *The Engraved Passion: New and Selected Poems 1970–1991* was published in 1991. He teaches at Goldsmiths College, University of London.

Medbh McGuckian (1950–) was born in Belfast. She has been writer-in-residence at Queen's University, Belfast, and visiting fellow at the University of California, Berkeley. Her collections include *The Flower Master and Other Poems* (1982), *Venus and the Rain* (1984), *On Ballycastle Beach* (1988) and *Marconi's Cottage* (1991).

Paula Meehan (1955–) was born in Dublin and studied at Trinity College, Dublin and at Eastern Washington University. Her collection *The Man who was Marked by Winter* (1991) was shortlisted for the *Irish Times*/Aer Lingus Irish Literature Prize for Poetry. *Pillow Talk* was published in 1994.

Máire Mhac an tSaoi (1922–) was born in Dublin, but spent most of her childhood in the west Kerry gaeltacht. She studied at University College, Dublin, became a scholar in the School of Celtic Studies at the Dublin Institute for

Advanced Studies, and later served in the Department of Foreign Affairs. Her collections include *Margadh na Saoire* (1956) and *An Galar Dubhach* (1980).

Edna St Vincent Millay (1892–1950) was born in Rockland, Maine and attended Vassar College. Her first volume of poetry, *Renascence*, was published in 1917. Her subsequent collections include *A Few Figs from Thistles* (1920), *The Buck in the Snow* (1928) and the posthumous *Mine the Harvest* (1954). From 1925 she lived on a farmstead in Austerlitz, New York, writing and supporting feminist and radical causes.

John Milton (1608–74) was born in London and studied at Cambridge. 'L'Allegro' and 'Il Penseroso' were written while he was still a student. A stay in Italy (he met Galileo) made a deep impression, but he was recalled to England by the outbreak of the Civil War. Milton became a staunch Parliamentarian and wrote a series of anti-episcopal pamphlets, including *Areopagitica* (1644). His greatest works are the epic poems *Paradise Lost* and *Paradise Regained* and the verse drama *Samson Agonistes*. Milton's gradual blindness became total in 1652.

John Montague (1929–) was born in Brooklyn, New York, of Irish parents, but grew up on his aunt's farm in County Tyrone. He studied at St Patrick's College, Armagh and at University College, Dublin. His collections include *The Rough Field* (1972), *A Slow Dance* (1975), *The Dead Kingdom* (1984) and *Mount Eagle* (1988). He has written fiction and essays, and has taught at several universities, in the United States and Ireland.

Marianne Moore (1887–1972) was born in St Louis, Missouri. She studied at Bryn Mawr College, and from 1921 to 1925 worked in the New York Public Library. In 1925 she became acting editor of *The Dial* and remained with the magazine until it ceased publication in 1929. Her collected writings contain several books of poems, critical essays and a translation of the fables of La Fontaine.

Thomas Moore (1779–1852) was born in Dublin and was one of the first Catholics to be admitted to Trinity College, Dublin. In 1799 he went to London, where his drawing-room singing and conversation made him an immediate success. He was befriended by Walter Scott and Byron (whose biography he wrote, and whose memoirs he burnt). His fame rests on his *Irish Melodies*, published in ten parts between 1808 and 1834, although his Persian tale in verse, *Lallah Rookh* (1817), won him critical and financial fortune.

Michael Moran (1794–1846), more usually known as Zozimus, was born in Faddle Alley in Dublin's Liberties. An illness blinded him when he was just a few weeks old. He became well known in the city as a balladeer and took the name of Zozimus, a fifth-century cleric, who discovered St Mary of Egypt when she was a hermit in the wilderness. The meeting of Zozimus and St Mary formed one of his favourite recitations.

Paul Muldoon (1951–) was born in County Armagh and grew up in The Moy, County Tyrone. He studied at Queen's University, Belfast. For several years he was a radio producer for the BBC in Belfast. He now teaches at Princeton University. His collections include *New Weather* (1973), *Why Brownlee Left* (1980), *Meeting the British* (1987) and *The Annals of Chile* (1994).

Richard Murphy (1927–) was born near Tuam, Co. Galway. His childhood was divided between Ireland, England and Ceylon. He studied at Oxford and at the Sorbonne. After several years of travel, he settled in Cleggan, Connemara, where he bought two Galway fishing hookers. Now he lives in Sri lanka and Killiney, Co. Dublin. He has lectured extensively in North America. His collections include *Sailing to an Island* (1963), *The Battle of Aughrim* (1968), *High Island* (1974) and *The Price of Stone* (1985).

Eiléan Ní Chuilleanáin (1942–) was born in Cork and studied at University College, Cork and at Oxford. Her first collection, *Acts and Monuments* (1972), won the Patrick Kavanagh Award. Since then, five more books have appeared: *Site of Ambush* (1975), *The Second Voyage* (1977, 1986), *The Rose-Geranium* (1981), *The Magdalene Sermon* (1989) and *The Brazen Serpent* (1994). She teaches Medieval and Renaissance English at Trinity College, Dublin.

Nuala Ní Dhomhnaill (1952–) was born in St Helen's, Lancashire and grew up in the west Kerry gaeltacht and north Tipperary. She studied at University College, Cork. She has lived in Holland, Turkey and Dublin. Her books include *An Dealg Droighin* (1981), *Féar Suaithinseach* (1984) and *Feis* (1991).

Máirtín Ó Direáin (1910–88) was born in Inishmore, Aran Islands, but left there in 1928 to work in the post office in Galway. He became involved in the Irish-language movement, especially the theatre. In 1938, the year in which he began writing poetry, he moved to Dublin and worked in the civil service. His collections include *Rogha Dánta* (1949), *Ó Mórna agus Dánta Eile* (1957) and *Dánta 1939–1979* (1980).

Dennis O'Driscoll (1954–) was born in Thurles, Co. Tipperary. His three collections are *Kist* (1982), *Hidden Extras* (1987) and *Long Story Short* (1993), and he is one of Ireland's most widely published critics of poetry. He works as a civil servant in Dublin.

Liam Ó Muirthile (1950–) was born in Cork and studied at University College, Cork. He has published two collections: *Tine Cnámh* (1984) and *Dialann Bóthair* (1992). He is a freelance writer and broadcaster; *An Peann Coitianta* (1991) is a selection of his weekly columns for *The Irish Times*.

Brian O'Nolan (1911–66), who wrote as Flann O'Brien and as Myles na gCopaleen, was born in Strabane, Co. Tyrone. He studied Celtic languages at University College, Dublin, and from 1935 to 1953 worked in the Department of Local Government. His 'Cruiskeen Lawn' column in *The Irish Times* was widely enjoyed. The most celebrated of his works of fiction are *At Swim-Two-Birds* (1939), *An Béal Bocht* (1941) and the posthumously published *The Third Policeman* (1967).

Seán Ó Ríordáin (1916–77) was born in Ballyvourney, Co. Cork and studied at North Monastery CBS. His collections are *Eireaball Spideoige* (1952), *Brosna* (1964) and *Línte Liombó* (1971). He worked in the motor taxation department of Cork Corporation and for some years wrote a weekly column in Irish for *The Irish Times*.

Frank Ormsby (1947–) was born in Enniskillen, Co. Fermanagh and studied at Queen's University, Belfast. His collections are *A Store of Candles* (1977) and *A Northern Spring* (1986) and he has edited several anthologies. He teaches at The Royal Belfast Academical Institution and is a former editor of *The Honest Ulsterman*.

Cathal Ó Searcaigh (1956–) was born in Meenala, Co. Donegal. He studied French, Russian and Irish at the National Institute for Higher Education in Limerick and later worked for RTÉ for a number of years. His collections include *Súile Shuibhne* (1983) and *Suibhne* (1987).

Seán Ó Tuama (1926–) was born in Cork and studied there at University College, where he was later Professor of Modern Irish Literature. He taught as a visiting professor at Harvard University and at Jesus College, Oxford. His three collections are *Faoileán na Beatha* (1962), *Saol fó thoinn* (1978) and *An Bás i dTír na nOg* (1988). His influence as writer, critic, teacher and mentor has been pervasive in modern writing in Irish.

Wilfred Owen (1893–1918) was born in Oswestry, Shropshire and studied at London University. He spent a year near Bordeaux as a tutor to two French boys, but returned to England and enlisted in the Lancashire Fusiliers. Invalided out of the Great War in 1917, Owen was sent to a war hospital where a fellow patient, Siegfried Sassoon, encouraged him to write poetry. Owen went back to the Front and was killed in action a week before the Armistice.

Boris Pasternak (1890–1960) was born in Moscow and studied philosophy at Moscow University and in Germany. His first collection of poems was published in 1914. Although he is known as a lyric poet and dramatist (he translated some of Shakespeare's plays), his most famous work is *Doctor Zhivago* (1957), an epic novel, for which he was awarded the Nobel Prize for Literature in 1958; adverse reaction in the Soviet Union led him to decline the award.

Tom Paulin (1949–) was born in Leeds and grew up in Belfast. He studied at the University of Hull and at Oxford. His books include *The Strange Museum* (1980), *Liberty Tree* (1983), *Fivemiletown* (1987) and *Walking a Line* (1994). He has edited two anthologies, and has adapted Sophocles' *Antigone* and Aeschylus' *Prometheus Bound*. He holds the G.M. Young Lectureship in English Literature at Hertford College, Oxford.

Craig Raine (1944–) was born in Sheldon, County Durham. He studied at Oxford and has lectured at the university. From 1981 to 1991 he was poetry editor at Faber and Faber. His books include *The Onion Memory* (1978), *A Martian Sends a Postcard Home* (1979), *Rich* (1984) and *History: The Home Movie* (1994). He is Fellow in English at New College, Oxford.

Theodore Roethke (1908–63) was born in Saginaw, Michigan and studied at the University of Michigan and at Harvard University. A selection of the poems from his first four books was contained in *Words for the Wind* (1957). He taught at various colleges in the United States. His last book, *The Far Field*, was published a year after his death.

Gabriel Rosenstock (1949–) was born in Kilfinane, Co. Limerick. Poet, playwright, children's author, translator and journalist, he is chairman of Poetry Ireland/Eigse Éireann and works with An Gúm, an Irish-language publisher. His collections include *Portrait of the Artist as an Abominable Snowman* (1989) and *Cold Moon* (1993).

Christina Rossetti (1830–94) was born in London and was educated at home. A devout Anglican, she gave much of her life to charitable works and the care of relatives. Like her brother, the poet Dante Gabriel Rossetti, she was associated with the Pre-Raphaelites, who sought refuge from the materialism of industrial Britain in the beauty and relative simplicity of the medieval world.

William Shakespeare (1564–1616) was born in Stratford-upon-Avon and attended the local grammar school. As a young man he moved to London where he became an actor and theatre manager. Here he wrote the thirty-seven plays for which he is known worldwide. By 1611 he had retired to Stratford. His sonnet sequence—154 poems in all—was written during the 1590s and was first published in 1609.

Percy Bysshe Shelley (1792–1822) was born in Horsham, Sussex. He studied at Oxford, but his collaboration in writing a pamphlet expounding atheistic beliefs caused his expulsion. In 1811 he married Harriet Westbrook, but three years later eloped with Mary Wollstonecraft and eventually married her. From 1818 he lived in Italy, where he composed the great body of his work, including *Prometheus Unbound* (1820) and *Adonais* (1821). He drowned while sailing on the Ligurian Sea.

161

Charles Simic (1938–) was born in Yugoslavia. He studied in the United States at the University of Chicago and at New York University. His collections include *What the Grass Says* (1967), *Dismantling the Silence* (1971) and *Unending Blue* (1981). He teaches at the University of New Hampshire.

Peter Sirr (1960–) was born in Waterford and studied at Trinity College, Dublin. He spent some years in Holland and Italy and now lives in Dublin where he is Director of the Irish Writers' Centre. His collections are *Marginal Zones* (1984), *Talk, Talk* (1987) and *Ways of Falling* (1991).

Iain Crichton Smith (1928–), born in Glasgow, was brought up on the Island of Lewis, Outer Hebrides. He attended Aberdeen University and taught English for twenty-two years, mostly in Oban High School. He has written poems, short stories and novels in Gaelic and English, and now lives in Taynuilt, Argyll.

Michael Smith (1942–) was born in Dublin. His collections include *Times & Locations* (1972), *Stopping to Take Notes* (1980) and *Lost Genealogies & Other Poems* (1993). He has translated work by Machado, Neruda, Vallejo and Lorca, and is the publisher of New Writers' Press.

Stevie Smith (1902–71) was born Florence Margaret Smith in Hull, Yorkshire. She was brought up in Palmers Green, London and lived most of her life with an aunt. She worked in publishing for more than thirty years. Her fiction includes *Novel on Yellow Paper* (1936), but she is mainly known for her poetry, much of it illustrated with her own line-drawings.

Wallace Stevens (1879–1955) was born in Reading, Pennsylvania. He spent most of his adult life in Hartford, Connecticut, working as a lawyer for the Hartford Accident and Indemnity Company, of which he became vice-president in 1934. His first collection, *Harmonium*, was published in 1923. Later books included *The Man with the Blue Guitar* (1937) and *Notes Toward a Supreme Fiction* (1942).

Anne Stevenson (1933–) was born in Cambridge, England, of American parents, but she grew up in the United States. She has taught in both countries. Her collections include *Travelling Behind Glass* (1974), *Enough of Green* (1977) and *The Other House* (1990). Her biography of Sylvia Plath, *Bitter Fame*, was published in 1989.

Robert Louis Stevenson (1850–94) was born in Edinburgh and studied at Edinburgh University. He was afflicted by a severe respiratory illness and in 1873 sought a healthier climate on the French Riviera. He travelled in France and wrote *Travels with a Donkey in the Cevennes* (1879). His most famous books are *Treasure Island, A Child's Garden of Verses, Kidnapped, The Strange*

Case of Dr Jekyll and Mr Hyde and *The Master of Ballantrae*. Late in life he settled in Samoa and was working on the unfinished *Weir of Hermiston* when he died.

John Millington Synge (1871–1909) was born in Rathfarnham, Co. Dublin and studied at Trinity College, Dublin. As a young man he lived in Germany and France. Two parts of Ireland—the West and County Wicklow—absorbed his interest. Synge is known primarily as a playwright, especially for *The Playboy of the Western World* (1907), but he wrote prose works, as well as poetry.

Alfred, Lord Tennyson (1809–92) was born in Somersby, Lincolnshire, the son of a country rector. He studied at Cambridge, where he met Arthur Hallam, whose early death in 1833 prompted him to write his most famous poem, *In Memoriam*, published in 1850. That same year Tennyson was appointed Poet Laureate and he eventually became the most celebrated poet of the Victorian age.

Dylan Thomas (1914–53) was born in Swansea, Wales. He worked for a time as a reporter on the *South Wales Evening Post*. His first volume, *Eighteen Poems*, was published in 1934. Thomas worked for the BBC during the war and his play for radio, *Under Milk Wood* (1954), is the best-known of his writings. He died during a lecture tour of the United States.

Edward Thomas (1878–1917) was born in Lambeth, London, of Welsh parents. He won a scholarship to Oxford, married young, and supported his family by taking on writing commissions—travel books, studies of nature and critical biographies. He became friendly with Robert Frost, who encouraged him to write poetry. Thomas was killed at the battle of Arras with an edition of Shakespeare in his pocket.

R.S. Thomas (1913–) was born in Cardiff. He learned Welsh in adulthood and was ordained as a clergyman in the Church of Wales in 1936. He served in a number of parishes in mid- and north Wales until his retirement in 1978. His collections include *Song at the Year's Turning* (1955), *The Bread of Truth* (1963), *H'm* (1972) and *Experimenting with an Amen* (1986). His autobiography, *Neb*, was published in Welsh in 1985.

John Updike (1932–) was born in Shillington, Pennsylvania and studied at Harvard University and at the Ruskin School of Drawing and Fine Art in Oxford. During the mid-1950s he was on the staff of *The New Yorker*. He is best known as a novelist—*Rabbit, Run* (1960), *Couples* (1968), *Roger's Version* (1987), among others—and as a literary critic and essayist, but his first book was a collection of poetry and he subsequently wrote *Hoping for a Hoopoe* (1959) and *Telephone Poles and Other Poems* (1963).

163

Ruth Valentine (1945–) was born in London, where she works as a freelance management consultant for charities and voluntary organizations. Her collection of poems, *The Identification of Species*, was published in 1991.

Victor Vroomkoning (1938–) was born in Boxtel in The Netherlands, the son of a Belgian mother and a Dutch father. His first poems appeared in 1981 and he has published several collections since then. He is a teacher of Dutch and lives in Nijmegen.

Derek Walcott (1930–) was born in Castries, St Lucia and studied at the University of the West Indies. He became a schoolteacher, had his first collection of poems published in 1948 and subsequently wrote a series of verse dramas. His books include *The Fortunate Traveller* (1981), *Midsummer* (1984), *The Arkansas Testament* (1987) and *Omeros* (1990). He teaches at Boston University and divides his time between Boston and the Caribbean. In 1992 he was awarded the Nobel Prize for Literature.

Edmund Waller (1606–87) was born near Beaconsfield, Buckinghamshire. He studied at Eton and Cambridge and became a Member of Parliament when he was only sixteen. He supported Charles I in the Civil War and conceived a plot to secure the city of London for the king. When this was discovered, Waller was banished and he spent seven years in Paris. After the Restoration he again sat in Parliament, where he served until his death.

Walt Whitman (1819–92) was born on Long Island, New York. He left school in 1830 to be a printer's devil, and eventually became a full-time journalist. In 1855, at his own expense, he published a volume of twelve poems, *Leaves of Grass*, and continued to enlarge and revise further editions of this work until his death. His poetry on the American Civil War, found in *Drum-Taps* (1865), includes two well-known elegies for Abraham Lincoln. For the last eight years of his life, he lived alone, a semi-invalid, in Camden, New Jersey.

Richard Wilbur (1921–) was born in New York. He studied at Amherst College and Harvard University. During World War II he served in the American army in France and Italy. He has taught at several American universities and has translated Molière, Racine, Borges and Voznesensky. His books include *Things of This World* (1956), *Walking to Sleep* (1969), *The Mind-Reader* (1976) and *New and Collected Poems* (1988).

Oscar Wilde (1854–1900) was born in Dublin and studied at Trinity College, Dublin and at Oxford. *Poems* (1881) was his first published work. Ten years later his only novel, *The Picture of Dorian Gray*, appeared, but it was his five plays that made his name. In 1895 Wilde was imprisoned for two years for homosexual offences; he wrote *The Ballad of Reading Gaol* (1898) and the posthumous *De Profundis* (1905) while serving this sentence. After his release, he lived in France and Italy, plagued by ill health and bankruptcy.

William Carlos Williams (1883–1963) was born in Rutherford, New Jersey. After studying medicine at the University of Pennsylvania and in Leipzig, he spent his working life as a paediatrician and family doctor in his home town. At the same time he was in the forefront of avant-garde movements in the United States. His large output includes stories, plays, novels, a memoir, essays (*In the American Grain*), criticism, volumes of shorter poems, and *Paterson* (1946–58), a long epic poem.

Sheila Wingfield (1906–92) was the pen-name of Sheila, Viscountess Powerscourt. She was born in Hampshire, England. Drawn to the classics and mythology, she wrote five volumes of poetry and two memoirs. Her *Collected Poems* was published in 1983.

W.B. Yeats (1865–1939) was born in Sandymount, Dublin and spent his childhood and youth in Dublin, Sligo and London. He fell in love with the actress and nationalist Maud Gonne, who inspired much of his work. Yeats played a central role in the establishment of the Abbey Theatre in 1904. He was awarded the Nobel Prize for Literature in 1923 and was a member of Seanad Éireann from 1922 to 1928. His many collections include *The Wanderings of Oisin and Other Poems* (1889), *Responsibilities* (1914), *The Tower* (1928) and *The Winding Stair and Other Poems* (1933).

Acknowledgments

Those whose names lead all the rest are the poets.

The publishers, poets and translators of work still in copyright have kindly granted permission for it to be reprinted here:

Raphael Alberti, for 'Nana'; Benny Andersen, for 'Fotografierne'; Elizabeth Barrett, for Edna St Vincent Millay's 'First Fig'; The Blackstaff Press, for Padraic Fiacc's 'Vengeance' and John Hewitt's 'The Distances'; Bloodaxe Books, for Brendan Kennelly's 'Proof'; Joan Brossa, for 'Història'; John Calder (Publishers), for Samuel Beckett's 'Roundelay'; Jonathan Cape Ltd and the Estate of Robert Frost, for 'Fire and Ice'; Carcanet Press, for Eavan Boland's 'The Emigrant Irish', Iain Crichton Smith's 'Na hEilthirich' with its translation and William Carlos Williams's 'Flowers by the Sea'; Chatto and Windus, for Elizabeth Bishop's 'In the Middle of the Road'; R. Dardis Clarke, 21 Pleasants Street, Dublin 8, for Austin Clarke's 'Secrecy'; Elena Clementelli, for 'Di te non scriverò'; An Clóchomhar, for Máirtín Ó Direain's 'Ar Aíocht Dom' and for Seán Ó Tuama's 'Rousseau na Gaeltachta' and 'A Gaeltacht Rousseau'; M.J. Cohen, for J.M. Cohen's 'The Cocks'; Cló Iar-Chonnachta, for Cathal Ó Searcaigh's 'Seásúir'; The Dedalus Press, for Rory Brennan's 'The Oil Lamp', Denis Devlin's 'Boy Bathing' and Dennis O'Driscoll's '3 A.M.'; J.M. Dent, for Dylan Thomas's 'Once it was the colour of saying' and R.S. Thomas's 'The Bright Field'; Faber and Faber, for W.H. Auden's 'Gare du Midi', T.S. Eliot's 'Prelude I', Thom Gunn's 'The Bed', Randall Jarrell's 'A Lullaby', Philip Larkin's 'Talking in Bed', Louis MacNeice's 'Corner Seat', Marianne Moore's 'I May, I Might, I Must', Paul Muldoon's 'The Boundary Commission', Tom Paulin's 'Pot Burial', Theodore Roethke's 'Dolor', Wallace Stevens's 'Anecdote of the Jar', Derek Walcott's 'To Norline' and Richard Wilbur's 'Piazza di Spagna, Early Morning'; Brian Fallon, for Padraic Fallon's 'Body'; Peter Fallon, for Patrick Kavanagh's 'October'; Ian Hamilton Finlay, for 'au pair girl'; Forest Books, for Gabriel Rosenstock's 'Cléithin' and 'Splint'; The Gallery Press, for Brendan Behan's 'Uaigneas' and its translation, Ciaran Carson's 'Two Winos', Gerald Dawe's 'To My Inhaler', Seamus Deane's 'Scholar', Seán

Dunne's 'Throwing the Beads', Michael Hartnett's 'Fís Dheireanach Eoghain Rua Uí Shuilleabháin' and its translation, Dermot Healy's 'The Five Senses', Aidan Mathew's 'The Death of Irish', Medbh McGuckian's 'My Mother', Paula Meehan's 'Mrs Sweeney', Eiléan Ní Chuilleanáin's 'Pygmalion's Image', Liam Ó Muirthile's 'Sa Chaife', Frank Ormsby's 'Under the Stairs' and Peter Sirr's 'Their Laughter'; Farrar, Straus & Giroux, for Louise Bogan's 'Last Hill in a Vista'; Oliver D. Gogarty, SC, for Oliver St John Gogarty's 'Liffey Bridge'; HarperCollins, for e.e. cummings's 'Buffalo Bill's'; Seamus Heaney, for 'Dublin 4'; Mrs Iremonger, for Valentin Iremonger's 'Frozen'; Thomas Kinsella, for 'A bird is calling from the willow' and 'There are established personal places'; Alfred A. Knopf Inc., for Anthony Hecht's 'Retreat'; Anise Koltz, for 'Les oiseaux continuent à chanter'; Mrs Gweno Lewis, for Alun Lewis's 'Post-script: for Gweno'; James MacGibbon, for Stevie Smith's 'Not Waving But Drowning'; Hugh Maxton, for 'Thought of Dedalus'; Thomas McCarthy, for 'Seasons'; Máire Mhac an tSaoi, for 'Cré na Mná Tí' and 'The Housewife's Credo'; John Montague, for 'Border Lake' and 'The birds will still sing'; Richard Murphy, for 'Double Negative'; John Murray (Publishers) Ltd, for George Mackay Brown's 'Taxman'; Catherine O'Brien, for 'I will not write of you'; Dennis O'Driscoll and Peter van de Kamp, for 'Rubbish Bags'; Eoghan Ó hAnluain, for 'In the Café'; Sairséal Ó Marcaigh, for Seán Ó Ríordáin's 'Reo'; Mrs Evelyn O'Nolan, for Brian O'Nolan's 'The Tired Scribe'; Oxford University Press, for Joseph Brodsky's 'A Part of Speech', Derek Mahon's 'A Dying Art', Clarence Brown and W.S. Merwin's translation of Osip Mandelstam's 'Heaviness and tenderness' and Anne Stevenson's 'The Demolition'; Polygon Books, for Liz Lochhead's 'Fin'; David Pryce-Jones, for Sheila Wingfield's 'A Melancholy Love'; Penguin Books, for Geoffrey Hill's 'Merlin' and John Updike's 'Mirror'; Craig Raine, for 'Night Train'; Raven Arts, for Philip Casey's 'Lovers', Anthony Cronin's 'Sonnet 15', Michael Davitt's 'Leannain' and Nuala Ní Dhomhnaill's 'Gaineamh Shúraic'; Susan Schreibman, for 'History'; Secker and Warburg, for Michael Longley's 'Frozen Rain'; Charles Simic, for 'Fear'; Michael Smith, for 'Asleep in the City' and 'Lullaby'; Alexander Taylor, for 'Photographs'; Ruth Valentine, for 'Variations on a Theme of Chardin'; Victor Vroomkoning, for 'Vuilniszakken'; A.P. Watt, for Robert Graves's 'She Tells Her Love While Half Asleep'.

Every effort has been made to trace copyright holders. The publishers would appreciate being alerted to material included without permission.

Raymond Kyne was one of the founders of Poetry in Motion and his design of Poems on the DART has been decisive in the success of the venture.

167

James and Marianne Mays were also partners in Poetry in Motion from the beginning and have made a major contribution to the scheme.

Eoghan Ó hAnluain was of key importance in the selection of poems in Irish and has been a valued advisor.

Poems on the DART could have not come about without the support of Iarnród Éireann: special thanks to Cyril Ferris, Mary Linehan and the maintenance staff in Fairview depot.

We acknowledge the generous encouragement of Poems on the Underground and warmly thank Judith Chernaik, Cicely Herbert and Gerard Benson.

Poetry in Motion is grateful to the following for their co-operation: Rory Brennan, Gerald Dawe, Mari-aymone Djeribi, Seán Dunne (who gave us the book's title), George Evans, Peter Fallon, Antony Farrell, Gillespie Screen Print Ltd, Laurence Henson, Ruth Jacob, Hugo Jellett, Micheal Johnston, Benedict Kiely, Ross Kyne, Mary Lavin, Roger Little, Michael Lynam, Ray Lynn, David Marcus, Muriel McCarthy, Bertha McCullagh, Nuala O'Faoláin, Rory O'Neill, Lithe Sebesta, Stephen Wilson and Michael B. Yeats.

Index of titles

169

Index of poets and translators

173

Index of first lines

176